The Leices...   ...und
A walking ...

CW00509238

The Leicestershire Ro...   [
without members of the   ɔ
were inspired to create ...   's
centenary in 1987. To those who produced ...   ıd
to current members who help maintain and promote the walk we
are most grateful. With so many involved over the years there will
be no individuals named.

Thanks to those outside LFA who have allowed use of their pictures in this guide, Jean Harrison, Gordon Crook and members of the Countesthorpe U3A Photographic Group.

We are in debt to Leicestershire County Council for their continued support for the Leicestershire Round on the ground and with past publications.

To Carol and Sue at Words and Graphics for their patience and co-operation.

All map extracts copied from Ordnance Survey mapping are © Crown copyright and database rights 2014. O.S. Licence 100058392

ISBN: 978-1-5272-0622-9

INTRODUCTION

Welcome to the third guide to The Leicestershire Round. This long distance walk encircling Leicester was devised by members of the Leicestershire Footpath Association (LFA) to mark the centenary of their organisation in 1987. One hundred miles mark one hundred years.

The route takes in some of the highlights of Leicestershire, Charnwood Forest, Bradgate Park, Burrough Hill Iron Age Fort, Foxton Locks, Burbage Common and Bosworth Battlefield Centre. It visits many pretty villages, varied countryside and passes through a part of the National Forest.

While you may be inspired to take on the challenge of the full distance, the walk can be broken down into attractive and interesting day walks. There is also the option to make circular walks using a part of the route.

The Round is on the doorstep of a large urban population including Leicester, Loughborough, Melton Mowbray, Market Harborough, Hinckley and Coalville. The section from Barwell to Frisby on the Wreake (40 miles) is especially easy to access by bus.

The route has always had the support of Leicestershire County Council (LCC) and is well maintained by them with the installation of gates, yellow topped posts and ditch crossings. The route is shown as a Recreational Route on Ordnance Survey (OS) maps. Distinctive waymarking is now carried out by wardens, co-ordinated by the LFA. All this aids navigation allowing you to enjoy the surroundings. This guide also offers information about interest along the way.

The first guide did not reach the top of Langton Caudle. That was added in the 1996 guide. This guide makes a few more changes for safety and enjoyment but, beware, the footpath network is ever changing so check for updates online.

THE LEICESTERSHIRE ROUND

The 100 mile route takes you in a clockwise direction around the county of Leicestershire, through a wide variety of scenery from the rugged rocky area of Charnwood, through the wide river valleys of the Wreake and the Soar up to the high and windy ridges of East Leicestershire and Rutland. We cross the land where the Iron Age people chose to build their hill fort at Burrough Hill and then descend to lower slopes where many small streams feed the rich clay arable fields. Our path goes over the low hills of the Langtons with views over the rich pastures of the wide Welland valley.

We gradually swing west to reach Foxton's famous staircase of locks before moving uphill over to wooded hills of Gumley and Saddington, crossing the south of the county to High Cross, the Roman centre of England, where Watling Street crosses the Fosse Way. From here the old Fosse Way makes for pleasant, quiet walking. Going northwards towards Bosworth Field you join the Ashby canal for a short distance and pass through the historic market town of Bosworth and the village of Shackerstone with its impressive 12th century castle mound. From there the land once more rises and you pass over former mining country, now part of the National Forest, to reach the outskirts of Charnwood passing Thornton Reservoir and thence back to Newtown Linford where the walk begins and ends.

HISTORY OF THE GUIDES

This is a totally rewritten guide and is published thirty years after the original launch. Although the walk was created to celebrate the centenary in 1987, the work was approached with such enthusiasm that the first part of the guide appeared in 1981. That guide was produced by LFA members in three small brown covered booklets starting at Burrough Hill, Foxton Locks and Market Bosworth. Each sold at just £0.75p. They were published by the Leicestershire Libraries Service, with illustrations by Jean Harrison and hand drawn maps. Some of the sketches have been reproduced in this guide.

The second guide of 1996 with a revised re-print in 2011 was produced in house by Leicestershire County Council. It covered the whole route in a single pocket sized book. It had more local interest information but still had hand drawn maps and sketches.

It has been interesting to note changes along the way. Most noticeable has been the number of church towers and spires now hidden from view by trees, no longer of use to us as navigational aids. Planting in the National Forest has made huge changes with field boundaries and open views lost, replaced by well-defined paths and wildlife. Fences to be climbed have gone, so have many stiles replaced by easy access gates. The network of paths will continue to change so please note this guide can only be correct at the time of writing.

WALKING THE LEICESTERSHIRE ROUND

The ten sections described in the guide are based on the belief that a long distance rambler can comfortably manage on average ten miles in a day. A group of say four or five walkers could take two cars to cover each section. Some B&B and camping is mentioned in the text but a search of the web will offer the current accommodation.

The sections are then subdivided into village hops so that you could take your time to explore further. Elsewhere there are circular walks available if you need to return to your car.

Barwell to Frisby on the Wreake can easily be tackled as linear walks using public transport from Leicester. Melton Mowbray makes a good centre for buses to cover Frisby to Somerby. See Traveline for bus times.

The maps are at a scale of 1:25,000 from Ordnance Survey data. North is always top so as you walk around the circle the direction of travel along the maps can be left to right, top to bottom, right to left or bottom to top. Follow the arrows on the red highlight.

Although we have included some village services in the guide you should check they are still open and when they are open should you plan to use them. A better bet is to take a packed lunch and in hot weather plenty of liquid.

We have received reports of hardy folk tackling the Round in a single walk / jog. So far we haven't heard that it has been achieved within 24 hours. That could be your honour.

This guide and signs on the ground should make your walk straightforward but care is needed perhaps through villages, where waymarking is absent and across large arable fields. By law a path across ploughed land should be kept clear and there has been much improvement in recent years. If you find a problem along the way please bring it to the attention of either Leicestershire County Council or LFA. Both have contact details online. (Note: A short section of the route, Launde to Belton, is now in Rutland. LCC are not responsible here so pass your concerns to LFA.)

However you choose to approach the Leicestershire Round we invite you to follow the Country Code and enjoy what the countryside of Middle England has to offer.

INDEX

8. Roman High Cross (11 ½ miles)		81
Frolesworth – Claybrooke Parva	2 miles	82
Claybrooke Parva – High Cross	1 ½ miles	84
High Cross – Sharnford	2 ½ miles	86
Sharnford – Burbage	3 miles	88
Burbage – Barwell	2 ½ miles	91

9. Bosworth Field (11 miles)		93
Barwell – Sutton Wharf	3 ½ miles	94
Sutton Wharf – Sutton Cheney	2 miles	96
Sutton Cheney – Market Bosworth	2 miles	98
Market Bosworth – Shackerstone	3 ½ miles	100

10. National Forest (11 ½ miles)		105
Shackerstone – Nailstone	3 miles	105
Nailstone – Bagworth	2 miles	108
Bagworth – Thornton	1 ½ miles	109
Thornton – Markfield	2 miles	111
Markfield – Newtown Linford	3 miles	113

ROCKY CHARNWOOD
(8 miles)

NEWTOWN LINFORD - MOUNTSORREL

The section begins gently enough along the drive through Bradgate Park from Newtown Linford before climbing to Old John, the monument on the rocky hill, then down to Hunts Hill car park where there are toilets and ice cream vans in the summer season. Here you leave the tourists and stride across country from the high ground of the park, past rocky outcrops and patches of woodland and over a golf course to reach Woodhouse Eaves.

From Woodhouse Eaves the route crosses less hilly ground and skirts the lovely Swithland reservoir and the much damaged Buddon Hill. The sight and sound of steam trains will add to the atmosphere.

NEWTOWN LINFORD - WOODHOUSE EAVES
(4 miles)

NEWTOWN LINFORD *is an attractive and popular village only five miles from Leicester, there are facilities for the many visitors. Here you can admire thatched cruck cottage, houses with Swithland slate roofs and walk around the church with its fine Swithland slate gravestones. The car park at the entrance to Bradgate Park is open until dusk, it is therefore only useful to day walkers.*

BRADGATE PARK

This old deer park was once part of the Manor of Groby. The River Lin flows beside the main track and as you walk along you will almost certainly see deer browsing on the far side of the river. Ancient gnarled and hollow oaks are all around. The oldest tree to have been accurately dated is from 1595 but some of the trees may have been planted earlier when the house was built and would have been ready for pollarding in 1554. This fits with the tradition that the oaks were 'beheaded' at the same time as Lady Jane Grey, the young 'nine days' Queen of England. This is a sad story. As you walk through the park you will pass the ruins of the fine brick house built for the Greys of Groby and which was once the home of Lady Jane Grey. She was a direct descendant of Henry VII and when Edward VI died in 1554, at just 16 years old she was used by her family against her will to lay claim to the throne. After being Queen for nine days she was thrown into the tower, accused of treason and beheaded by order of Mary Tudor who then became queen. Although initially the Grey family lands were confiscated, after Queen Elizabeth's death, Henry Grey became 1st Earl of Stamford. The land stayed in the family until Lady Stamford, sold it in 1926 to Charles Bennion. He generously donated it to the people of Leicestershire for their enjoyment. It is now in the control of the Bradgate Park Trust.

Recent work done by the University of Leicester Archaeological Service revealed the presence here of hunter-gatherers from the Late Upper Palaeolithic Period, some 14,700 years ago. This was a time of rapid climate change. The ice sheets that had covered most of northern Europe began to retreat as the Earth warmed. Herds of animals began to move northwards to find new grazing and they were followed by intrepid bands of humans. The site at Bradgate gives us a fascinating snapshot of the lives of these people and the ways in which they adapted to a changing climate with the consequent impact on the herds of game on which they relied. Finds recovered from the site consist of flint tools and projectile points along with the debris from flint-knapping.

The Park is also of great interest because of its geology which ranges from the oldest Precambrian rocks in England to the youngest (Quaternary). The fossils at Bradgate are the only known Precambrian fossils in Western Europe. Until 1957 it had been thought that complex life forms and perhaps life itself began with the Cambrian Period and that all rocks older than this developed in a world without plants or animals. The 1957 discoveries by Roger Mason, in rocks near Woodhouse Eaves, required a re-evaluation of when life began. These fossils are now displayed in the New Walk Museum.

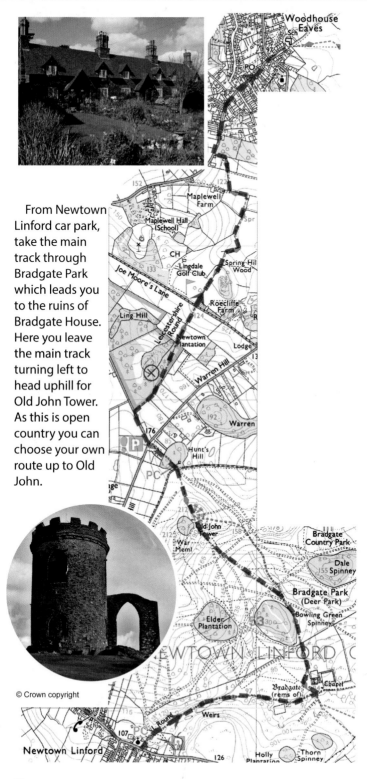

From Newtown Linford car park, take the main track through Bradgate Park which leads you to the ruins of Bradgate House. Here you leave the main track turning left to head uphill for Old John Tower. As this is open country you can choose your own route up to Old John.

© Crown copyright

This beer mug shaped monument was built as a folly in 1784. The toposcope was donated by the villagers of Newtown Linford using proceeds from their pageant in 1953. It indicates the distant landmarks which can be seen from the hill including Bardon Hill, the highest point in Leicestershire, at 278 metres.

From the monument keep in a north westerly direction and descend to the park gates at the foot of the hill. Continue through the car park at Hunts Hill, cross the road, and continue towards Shepshed on the road opposite (Benscliffe Road). After about 200 metres along the verge, turn right into Rough Hill Woodland. Follow the track taking the left fork (⊗ SK 52353 12135) which drops downhill to a gate. The gate gives access to Lingdale golf course, cross this to reach the road (Joe Moore's Lane).

Cross the road carefully to continue in the same direction beside the golf course, close to the hedge on your right. The route across the golf course is well signed. In the corner of the field, beside the fairway, pass the rocky outcrop of Spring Hill Wood on your right. You need to keep in the same direction, but make a detour right. Finally keep the hedge on your left until you come to the stile and slate bridge. Here you leave the golf course and enter a field corner with Maplewell Farm in the far left corner.

The path now follows the field boundary to your right, move round two sides of the field to the corner to the right of Maplewell farm buildings. (A well walked path crosses the grass field diagonally). Pass under the wires, cross the stile and follow the track, with the hedge on your left. Keep in the same direction, joining the gravel track from Barn Farm. This bends left to meet Maplewell Road, where you turn right to walk downhill into Woodhouse Eaves.

BROOMBRIGGS

On your left as you walk down Maplewell Road is a path leading to Broombriggs Farm. Donated to Leicestershire County Council in 1970 by the Frear family, the objective was to preserve its natural beauty as a typical Charnwood Forest farm. Permissive footpaths allow exploration of the fields and provide a short cut to Beacon Hill. (See Short Walks on the Leicestershire Round)

© Crown copyright

WOODHOUSE EAVES is an attractive little village of Charnwood granite and Swithland slate. It has several pubs for refreshment. There are shops, a post office, and a church built at the time of the enclosures on a rock over an old quarry. There is also a reasonable bus service and toilets in the recreation ground car park. The village became a popular tourist destination from the late 19th century. Numerous items of Goss and Devon Ware crested souvenir china were sold by the village Post Office.

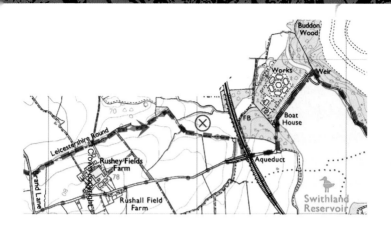

WOODHOUSE EAVES - MOUNTSORREL
(4 miles)

From the bottom of Maplewell Road cross the road junction and continue along Meadow Road. The path continues as a grass track to the right of the primary school. After a few yards the track enters a ploughed field, turn half right on a well walked path across the field towards the tall silos in the distance and a hedge corner. Walk with this hedge on your right to meet the road. Cross straight over the road and follow the headland with the hedge on your left. Continue in this direction for five fields, passing the buildings and silos of Rushey Fields Farm uphill to your right, and heading towards Buddon Hill. Cross two concrete farm tracks and continue close to the hedge on your left.

The Great Central railway line lies between you and Buddon Hill. The path which formerly led straight to the ancient settlement on Buddon Hill is deflected by the railway and now swings right to meet the railway crossing at Rabbits Bridge. At the end of the fifth field move to your right and keep close to the hedge on your left. From a gate in the corner of the next field (⊗ SK 55038 14505) you need to cross an open field. Pass close to the isolated oak tree and continue towards the railway line, passing a small water treatment building. Cross the concrete cart bridge and turn right to walk uphill close to the railway line. Meet the lane and turn left to cross Rabbits Bridge, pausing to wave at steam trains passing below.

This is the Great Central Railway, a late 19th century dream to link Manchester and Paris via a channel tunnel. Dr Beeching axed the line which closed in 1969 but enthusiasts have resurrected it and steam trains again pass under the bridge on a regular basis.

13

You now have a mile and a half of tarmac road walking along the pleasant Kinchley Lane, passing close to an expanse of water on your right.

Swithland reservoir opened in 1896 to serve the city of Leicester with a capacity of 500 million gallons. It soon became inadequate and a pipe line from Derbyshire's Derwent reservoirs was needed early in the 20th century. The lane skirts Buddon Wood on your left which was quarried for mill stones in the early Iron Age. This is a good time to admire the scenery, the woodland and the water birds on the reservoir. From this point you may see the steam trains crossing the viaduct.

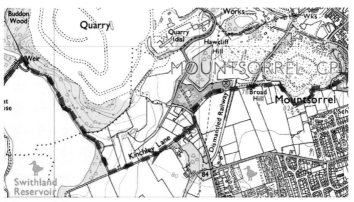
© Crown copyright

Follow the lane down to cross the reservoir dam, passing the fine Victorian buildings and the landscaped water gardens on your left. The lane bends right at the overflow channel and goes past Buddon Wood.

Eventually the road turns sharp left and goes uphill, with views of the huge quarried hill, now being reclaimed for grass and trees, over to your left. Pass Kinchley House on your right and granite cottages, near the old, small quarry site of Nunckley Hill.

Meet the road and turn left for a short distance (signs point to Stonehurst Farm Centre). Pass the end of Rushey Lane on your left and turn right along Bond Lane. Go slightly downhill on the road between bracken and gorse. This is Mountsorrel Common now sadly destroyed by quarry and landfill. Cross the bridge over the old mineral line (⊗ SK 57230 14725), recently re-opened as the Mountsorrel Branch of the Great Central Railway. When the road bends left just after the railway bridge turn right to go along a farm track. Follow the farm track, keeping close to the quarry landfill site over to your left.

Keep close to the quarry boundary wire as it swings left. Pass pony paddocks and small holdings on your right. Mountsorrel comes into view down on your right. The beacon and war memorial stand on the hill ahead.

At the track end take the road opposite. (A little way down here you can if you wish follow a path up steps to the memorial, go over the top of the hill and descend by steps and path into Mountsorrel.) Or continue on the road which becomes Watling Street, past the houses going steeply downhill to reach the old A6 by the Buttercross.

MOUNTSORREL

Once an impressive castle from the 12th century stood high on the hill overlooking the Wreake valley. What remained has now been quarried away in the interests of high quality road stone.

There are several shops and pubs at the foot of the steep castle hill. Various other establishments by the waterside include bed and breakfast. The town became prosperous in the 16th century as the many impressive houses indicate. The Buttercross, a domed rotunda, was built in 1793 to replace the old market cross, which now stands in Swithland Hall grounds.

Mountsorrel granite quarry has been in operation for at least 250 years according to current owners, Tarmac. The transport boom in the second half of the 18th century created a demand for granite cobbles, kerbs and chipping which were taken away by barge on the canal and today by rail. A recent planning application has extended the life of the quarry to 2040.

MOUNTSORREL - FRISBY

This section goes through an area liable to flooding. You are warned to avoid the riverside plains in periods of sustained wet weather.

Our route goes from the Soar over the high land near Ratcliffe on the Wreake, past Ratcliffe College, and down to its tributary the Wreake. The place names of the pretty villages of Rearsby, Hoby, Rotherby and Frisby on the Wreake which we pass through, as well as Brooksby which we see nearby, and Gaddesby, Ashby Folville, and Somerby show, with their endings "- by", that these villages were established or taken over by the Danes in Anglo Saxon times. The Danes travelled upriver from the sea, along the Trent, the Soar and the Wreake valleys to settle here in the 9th century. In the time of King Alfred, Leicestershire was part of the Danelaw, governed by Danish invaders.

MOUNTSORREL - COSSINGTON
(2 ½ miles)

Leaving Mountsorrel the route has been amended from earlier guides. The new route is a more pleasant and easier alternative.

From the Buttercross in the centre of Mountsorrel go north along Market Place then, opposite St Peters Church, turn right onto Sileby Road. At The Waterside Inn turn right past the lock on your right and follow the navigable River Soar along the towpath. This passes under the A6 bypass and over a branch of the river on a footbridge. A further footbridge takes the path over the main river and along the other bank. The Sileby Marina and Mill building are on the opposite bank.

Turn left to pass over the footbridge at the tail of the lock (**X** SK 59260 14740). Here you meet the original route. Cross another bridge with the weir on your right then, after a gate, turn sharp right to walk close to the canalised River Soar on your right for about half a mile. The path enters Cossington Meadows.

Cossington Meadow is managed by the Leicestershire and Rutland Wildlife Trust. The area occupied by the nature reserve was quarried for gravel during the 1980s and 90s while the Leicestershire Round was being devised. The pits were then filled with inert waste and some parts covered with soil and seeded with grass. Other areas were left with deep holes to form lakes. Interpretation boards around the site offer information about the plants and animals that have colonised the reserve.

© Crown copyright

19

Continue along the river bank to a field boundary hedge and yellow post, here turn left to follow the hedge on your left. Continue in this direction, crossing other waymarked paths until reaching the boundary of the reserve where you must bear right to exit the reserve. Continue close to the stream on your left and then along the enclosed track. Turn left at the gate and enter into a field with a hedge on your right to reach the memorial cross on the main street of Cossington. The church is hidden by trees on your right.

COSSINGTON *almost certainly has Saxon origins, the name being derived from the Saxon Chief Coss or Cussa. Lord Kitchener's father lived at the Manor House and is buried here. Lady Isobel Barnett, an early television personality, lived in the village. Much of the village along Main Street was designated a Conservation Area in 1975 hence it has some pleasant buildings. The Royal Oak is on Main Street just beyond our turning at Bennett's Lane.*

COSSINGTON - REARSBY
(4 miles)

© Crown copyright

Turn right to follow the main street of Cossington, then turn left along Bennetts Lane. This swings right to meet Back Lane. Turn left and follow Back Lane uphill over the busy main line railway bridge, then turn left along Blackberry Lane. This begins as a metalled road and continues as a green lane, past farm buildings, going rather muddily uphill to meet the main road. Cross over the Ratcliffe Road to continue in the same direction along the metalled drive to Elms Farm.

RATCLIFFE COLLEGE, *a co-ed Catholic public school was founded in 1847. The original Victorian Gothic buildings were designed by Augustus Welby Pugin. Past pupils include American actor Patrick McGoohan who co-created and starred in 'The Prisoner'.*

From this lane there are fine views back towards Mountsorrel, across the Soar Valley and over to Charnwood. Pass a grand Holme Oak (Quercus ilex – the evergreen oak) and the farm buildings on your right. A gate leads back into the college grounds Continue along the drive to the last house on the right 'Ambrose House' then turn right.

Cross the playing fields to the waymarked crossing in the hedge bearing slightly to your left. Continue diagonally over the next field now planted with young trees and keep in the same direction to reach the A46 Fosse Way. Cross very carefully going through the gap in the barrier of the central reservation to the waymark on the far side of the road slightly to your left. This involves a short walk along the verge towards oncoming traffic. Enter the field by the gate and walk downhill close to the hedge on your left. From a gate and footbridge in the corner a view of the Wreake valley is spread out in front of you. Rearsby lies ahead. Continue in the same direction across the ploughed field to the bottom left corner by a big ash tree. Turn left to reach Spinney Farm drive. Turn right to follow this tree lined tarmac farm drive. Meet the Thrussington Road, turn left and go round the sharp bend. Turn right onto a footpath across the field to join the drive to Rearsby Mill. Pass the beautiful mill pond and swing left to pass in front of the mill house.

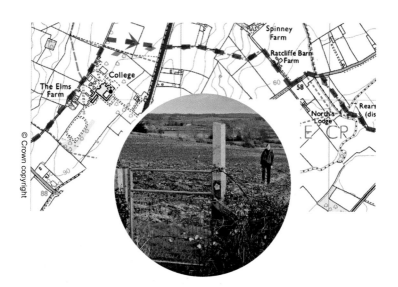

Many of the water mills we pass on the route are built on sites of previous mills constructed before the Norman Conquest and named in the Domesday Book.

Pack Horse Bridge, Rearsby

Cross the bridge over the river, then take the gate right to avoid Rearsby Mill Cottage over to your left. The path now moves away from the river. Another gate leads to a wide concrete bridge. Follow the green hedged lane which leads over the railway (a busy little line, which will get busier, so take care). The elegant slim

church tower of Rearsby comes into view over to the left. Pass a children's play park on your right. As the track bends left a narrow footpath provides the link to the road, or continue along the track to join Mill Road. Turn left, which leads into Brookside, Rearsby. Pass Manor Farm on your left and walk beside the stream. Pass various bridges finally arriving at a ford and the attractive granite packhorse bridge. The main part of the village lies to your right, on the main road.

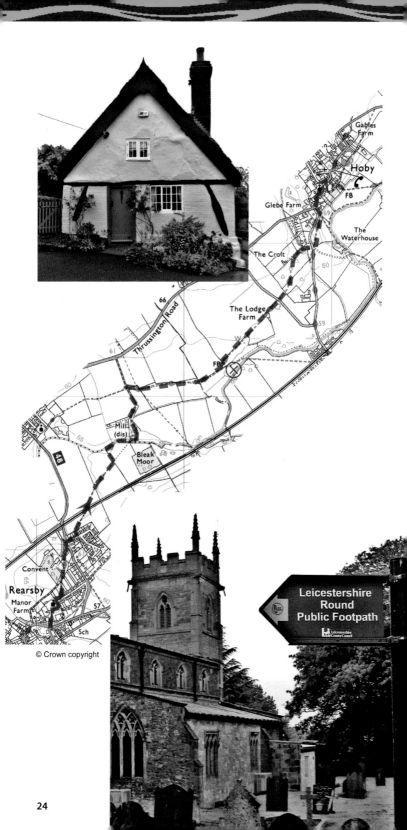

© Crown copyright

Leicestershire
Round
Public Footpath

Leicestershire
County Council

REARSBY

The seven arched packhorse bridge was built in 1714 while Pevsner says the bridge across the brook to the east of the church is 'certainly medieval'. On the other side of the bridge, in Mill Road there is a house of 1661 with an E-shaped gabled front, and the timber framed house nearby is dated 1613. There are two inns on the main road but no shop. Baker's Warden and Matteson produced the Rearsby Loaf, high in fibre and roughage for customers with tummy problems. Production transferred to Geary's of Ratby but it was discontinued in 2010.

REARSBY - HOBY
(2 ½ miles)

From Rearsby cross the packhorse bridge towards the church. Turn right at the top of Church Lane and follow the tarmac path which goes round two sides of the church wall to emerge on Church Leys Avenue. At number 22 turn left and go between the houses, through the kissing gate and turn right onto an open mown grassy area between the convent grounds to the left and mature chestnut trees. At the road turn left to go downhill and cross the road to walk along Wreake Drive. At number 7 turn left. A gate leads into the open field, move diagonally right across the ridge and furrow to the railway crossing.

Cross the railway line carefully. Thrussington church tower lies straight ahead but our route goes diagonally right to reach Thrussington Mill. Keep diagonally across two fields, but in the third turn left to follow the hedge on your left. Walk to the river side and then turn right, to keep close to the river on your left. Cross the brick bridge over the river and walk with it on your right then swing left onto the metal footbridge over the old lock.

Melton Mowbray Navigation was opened in 1797 linking the Soar Navigation with Melton Mowbray, a canalised River Wreake rather than being totally manmade. It closed in 1877 but some bridges and other structures remain. There were twelve locks in all and this bridge crosses the remains of Thrussington Mill Lock.

Continue along the enclosed path to pass the mill house and garden on your left. Cross the concrete cart bridge beside the old mill wheel housing (the marks of the old wheel are just about visible on the wall). Join the wooden sleeper path and continue along the mill access drive.

As you go along the drive, note cables and pylons on your left. At a wide gap in the hedges turn right into a field with a large pylon. Pass the pylon on your left and continue in the same direction across two fields to the corner of a projecting field. Here a gate provides access to the field recently planted with young trees. Keep the hedge on your left. After another gate the path enters meadow pasture. Continue with the hedge on your left. Ignore the disused brick bridge and the new footbridge on your right (⊗ SK 66275 16205). New buildings of Brooksby College are across the river. The spire of Hoby church comes into view. Head for this and the red brick house of Lodge Farm. Pass to the left of the house and follow the drive. Cross the road and continue straight across the open field. Move slightly left in the next two fields and pass an isolated house over to your left. Cross the cart bridge at the end of a line of trees and continue to the gate which leads you out onto the Brooksby-Hoby road. Cross this road and swing left in the field, keeping the road on your left. Cross old gravel hollows and rejoin the road. Continue uphill to the road junction and turn right to pass Hoby church on your left. Continue towards the Blue Bell Inn.

HOBY *is perched high up above the river and the 13th century church is built in soft ironstone. We pass a 15th century cruck cottage with its original roof tree still preserved. The chantry house has intriguing upper doors high up above the street. There is a village hall. The former school opposite closed in 1970 and is now a dwelling. The thatched Blue Bell Inn is open all day from noon and serves food mid-day and evenings.*

HOBY - FRISBY
(2 miles)

From Hoby take a metalled track down the right hand side of the village hall, between walls of houses to reach Back Lane (unsurfaced), where you turn left and then right. Walk steeply downhill on the fenced-off path. Cross the footbridge over the stream and go diagonally left across the big field to meet the river in the corner of the field, a good spot for kingfishers. Turn left and walk with the river on your right. Note various now useless bridges (this is the site of an old mill and another lock). Swing right and cross the long, arched footbridge spanning the river by the old weir.

The path forks here. Take the right fork keeping in the same direction, aiming for the left of the houses of Rotherby visible in the distance. Another double stile and bridge may be bypassed. Go through the railway hand gates and cross the line carefully.

Continue in the same direction close to the hedge on your right. In the top corner of the field cross the hedge and turn left with Rotherby village now behind you.

Keep the hedge on your left for two fields, and in the third field continue in the same direction, parallel with the hedge over to your right. Cross the stile to meet the road. In the field on the opposite side of the road walk close to the hedge on your right for three fields. The road moves away to the right but the footpath keeps in the same direction across pasture fields with interesting humps and hollows. Frisby church spire comes into view to guide you onward along a well walked path through pasture. Move slightly left towards a spinney, cross the stile and move slightly right towards a large cedar tree next to which is a gate. A gravel drive leads to Water Lane Frisby near the old village cross. The Bell Inn stands opposite, the village beyond is worth a little detour.

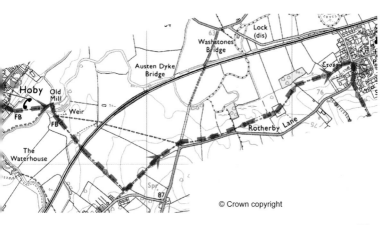

© Crown copyright

FRISBY church has a Norman tower base and a ten foot high market-cross stands opposite the Bell Inn on the village street. There is an ancient stump cross on the main road (A607). Frisby, originally settled on the Wreake for its importance as a trade route, lost its river traffic to the nearby railway, built in 1846. The village road was bypassed by the Turnpike road in 1810, leaving Frisby in a little backwater, below the busy Leicester-Melton road. There is still a shop, Post Office and internet café.

FRISBY - SOMERBY

This section is fairly strenuous. From Frisby we leave the Wreake valley and go up and over the gently rolling hills between the Wreake and Gaddesby brook. From Gaddesby our route climbs gradually to the high ground of Burrough Hill. The final climb up to the heights of Burrough Hill brings you out on the top of the Iron Age hill fort, with spectacular views over the countryside around. We cross the pasture land of the Burrough enclosure, descend quite steeply and then, after a gentle woodland track to Buttermilk Spinney, climb back to the rim of the Punch Bowl. From this ridge you walk over arable fields along well-trodden single-file tracks through crops to reach Somerby, a beautiful

ironstone village set in lovely parkland with horse pastures. Somerby provides limited bus service and refreshments. (The permissive path to Buttermilk Spinney is occasionally closed forcing a diversion and an extra mile.)

FRISBY - GADDESBY
(3 miles)

From Frisby leave Main Street and walk along Rotherby Lane passing the old market cross on your right. As the road swings right, turn left to cross the stile onto a narrow path and go uphill close to the hedge on your left. The hill flattens out and you meet the main A607 Melton-Leicester road, near the remains of the old cross stump. This is a busy and fast road, take care. Turn right then left across the road then continue in the same direction across a large field. In front of you lie the bands of low hills which you cross to reach Gaddesby. Go downhill at first, keeping parallel with a hedge over to your right. Pass close to a tree fringed pond (⊗ SK 69703 16835) on your right and make for the jutting out corner of a field in the dip. Continue uphill with the hedge a few metres away on your left. Over the brow of the hill the next crossing is near a big ash tree. Move slightly right across a narrow field to cross the footbridge. Go uphill over pasture to the top right corner of the field close to the 46M tall 50kW wind turbine at Frisby Grange (⊗ SK 69750 15808).

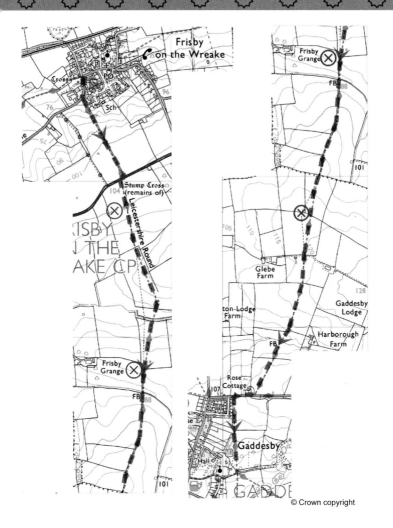

© Crown copyright

Continue downhill close to the hedge on your right. Cross the footbridge in the bottom right corner of the field and continue uphill to the top corner.

Enter a big open field, the path on the ground bears a little to the right off the definitive line across the field. Head for the yellow post (⊗SK 69548 14760). Bear slightly left from the post across the next field towards the crest of the hill. Cross the farm track and go straight across the next field and through the gate near the large tree. Continue downhill in the open field to a twin gate boundary and into pasture. Bear right across a small field to another twin gate and bridge. Cross another small field and in the next head for the far right corner where trees and a tall hedge hide the stile leading to the lane. Meet the road and turn right towards Gaddesby.

Just before the houses take the footpath left and follow the field edge path with houses to your right. The path passes into pasture with isolated parkland trees. Pass a lake on your right in the grounds of Gaddesby Hall which is hidden by new houses and finally meet a disused drive to Hall Farm away to the left.

Here you can turn right to visit Gaddesby church, village and The Cheney Arms.

GADDESBY

The followers of the Viking Gaddr settled on a south facing site above Gaddesby Brook. There is evidence that by the twelfth century a motte-and-bailey castle was built at Gaddesby on top of the hill. The Manor of Gaddesby was once owned by the Knights Templar of Rothley. There are springs and village pumps in Chapel Lane. At the corner of Chapel Lane and Cross Street there stands, but ignored, a large glacial Ice Age erratic (a piece of rock that differs from that native to the area), known locally as Blue Stone. This is remembered as the place from which Wesley preached when visiting friends in the village.

The present Gaddesby Hall was built in 1744 with additions in 1868 but then significantly reduced in size in the 1950s. It stands on the site of Paske Hall built in 1390. The 13th and 14th century limestone and ironstone church is generally reckoned to be the most beautiful in the county. The tall spire can be seen for miles. Inside are medieval benches which are early examples of wooden seating and box pews. The white marble monument to the Cheney family soldier who died at the battle of Waterloo is a dominant feature. It originally stood in the conservatory of the Hall but was moved when the estate was sold in 1917.

© Crown copyright

GADDESBY - ASHBY FOLVILLE
(1 mile)

Go straight across the drive, over a stile and then move diagonally left, going downhill to cross the corner of the field. Cross the footbridge and across the corner of a field to a gate. Climb steeply into an open arable field. Continue uphill in the same direction, making for the left side of the clump of trees and keep these on your right to the bottom left corner of the field. The well waymarked route now follows the valley, passing the disused windmill base at Mill Farm and the stream over to your right.

Keep in this direction, crossing the fenced Midshires Way bridle track (⊗ SK 69733 12703) and make for the stile in the corner of the field, near the stream, slightly to your right. Cross the open field and meet a hedge on your right. Keep in the same direction, and then move slightly left to pass a sewage works which is over to your right. Continue moving left uphill to reach the far left corner of the big field and the lovely tree-lined road into Ashby Folville from Great Dalby.

After crossing the road, move slightly right in the field and away from the hedge on your left. A line of houses lies ahead, with Ashby Folville church tower over to the right of them but lost now in the trees. Take the path between the houses and emerge on Highfield End, by a steep flight of brick steps. We bypass the village, but you can turn right here to go along the street to the Carington Arms pub, the church and the village cricket ground. Return to this point to continue.

The lovely name of ASHBY FOLVILLE indicates a Danish settlement, later given a Norman French family name. The "ash" part of the name is common for villages in places where ash trees grew, but it can also be from the Old Norse personal name of Aski.

Ashby Folville Manor is late 19th century Neo-Tudor style once home of the Smith-Caringtons. It is said that the late Duke of Windsor first met Mrs Simpson at a house party here. The family still own much of the village including the pub and the quintessential English cricket ground. The Smiths are descended from Sir Michael Carington, standard bearer to Richard Lionheart. In the church there are wall monuments to the Woodford family in the 14th century and tombs to the Smiths of 1607 and 1629. The most impressive monuments are in finest alabaster which came from Chellaston just north of the Trent, where schools of craftsmen flourished from 1334 to 1634. These tombs were made just before the quarries were exhausted.

ASHBY FOLVILLE - THORPE SATCHVILLE
(2 miles)

The path continues from the opposite side of Highfield End. Walk close to the hedge of the white house on your left and keep in the same direction, passing the protruding corners of hedges on your right. Ashby Folville is now over to your right in a woodland setting. Keep in the same direction across the big open fields, with the tree-lined stream over to your right. Pass close to the waymarked pole in the middle of the field and continue to the huge electricity pylon ahead (⊗ SK 71615 11970)

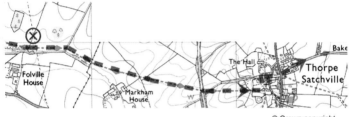

© Crown copyright

Pass over a concrete bridge close to another wooden pole to enter a large grass field. Bear left to pass under the wires. Markham House with large outbuildings is on your right. Head for the houses of Thorpe Satchville on the hill ahead and locate a stile in the far corner. Continue in the same direction, across the corner of one field and into the corner of a very large field. Continue in the same direction noting a large tree on the horizon and head to the left of this. On the brow of the hill a brick bridge will become apparent. Head for this and pass under the tree-lined former railway embankment. Entering a field bear left to climb the hill. A barn comes into view. Pass close to the right of this and continue towards the village. The path then skirts the ha-ha wall of The Elms on your left. Cross a stile and turn left to enter the churchyard.

Pass the little church of St. Michael and meet Church Lane. Turn right to meet the main B6047 Melton - Market Harborough Road, opposite Bakers Lane.

THORPE SATCHVILLE - BURROUGH HILL
(2 miles)

THORPE SATCHVILLE *village is impressively sited on the hill ridge. The steep sides of the rolling hills make fine pastures for horses and the area still forms part of the important Melton hunting scene. Thorpe Satchville was also a tennis Mecca. From 1896 when George and Blanche Hillyard settled here at The Elms (house with the ha-ha) on Church Lane just about every world class tennis player visited the village often before winning a title at Wimbledon.*

The Fox Inn closed in 2014. It once had walls papered with Ordnance Survey Maps. A later landlady gave it a French café flavour with red and white check table cloths and French food. The garage which occupied the former chapel has also closed. Only the village hall now offers some community cohesion. A millennium stone can be inspected after crossing the road. The former railway that you cross on approaching the village was built jointly by the

Great Northern and London North Western companies to break the dominance of the Midland Railway with coal traffic to London. This line had to take a route through remote countryside so stations provided for the small villages saw little trade.

Follow Bakers Lane for about a mile. Where the metalled road goes sharp left you turn off right. The next section has been damaged by off road recreation vehicles so take care down the steep rutted track of Salter's Hill. The route to Burrough Hill can be seen ahead of you extending as a well marked track up to the ramparts above the steep escarpment of the Iron Age hill fort.

Follow the track down to the Melton lane. Cross carefully and continue along the field road up to Burrough Hill. The track bends right at the top to cross through gates, here you have a choice. A short cut goes left to zig-zag up steep tracks between gorse bushes leading to the ramparts and toposcope. The alternative well marked track right takes the 'low route' round the edge of the hill and leads to the 'front entrance', the car park, picnic site with toilets. You then need to double back to admire the view. The toposcope indicates viewpoints such as Billesdon Coplow and Whatborough Hill. Pause to take in the view and history of this location.

BURROUGH HILL *is an Iron Age fort which occupies a promontory and commands a wide view of the Wreake valley. A recent excavation has uncovered decorated bronze remains from an Iron Age chariot. The site has long been used as a place of recreation. Leland, keeper of the Kings Library in the 16th century, who travelled the country recording for Henry VIII the antiquities held in various important buildings, writes 'to these Borow Hills every year on Monday after Whit Sunday come people of the country there about, and shoot, run, wrestle, dance, and use like other feats of exercise'. The historian Burton, a century later, states that such sports used to take place, but*

they had apparently been discontinued in his day. They were revived later and again abandoned in the 18th century. In the early 19th century the Melton Hunt established a race meeting at Burrough on the Wednesday after the second Sunday in June (Nicholls, Leicestershire ii 524) these races were held until about 1870. The land, owned by the Ernest Cook Trust, is now administered as a country park by the Leicestershire County Council for the enjoyment of all and you are more likely to see families flying kites or wandering through the woods. At Burrough Hill there are many ancient public footpaths, as you would expect in an area long settled and so popular with visitors, both for its historical interest and its marvellous position and views. Leicestershire County Council has negotiated agreements for access to the public to many parts of the hill and the Ernest Cook Trust has opened a permissive path along the Dalby Hills. It is important to note that this path is unfortunately only a permissive path. It is not marked on O.S. maps and it can be closed at any time and is usually closed on Thursdays in the shooting season. You are asked to take care to respect the use of the path by others and to use the road detour when dangerous activities take place. A notice board informs you when the path is closed.

BURROUGH HILL - SOMERBY
(2 - 3 miles)

This section is fairly strenuous and is approximately 3 miles using the Ernest Cook Trust permissive path (check the board for closures), or the blue line on the map, 4 miles via the road to Little Dalby if the permissive path is closed.

From the toposcope, continue clockwise inside the Burrough Hill enclosure, close to the northern rampart on your left. Go through a slight dip in the ramparts just to the right of the curved corner. From this point look across the steep valley, a line of fencing descends the hill and rises to a fenced gateway ($\otimes$ SK 76300 12228) halfway up the hill. You can go steeply down and up to this point or wind your way more sedately on zig zag tracks.

© Crown copyright

Go through the fence gates and follow the green path along the contour of the Dalby Hills until you meet the notice board which informs you whether the permissive path is open or not. If the path is open, follow it for half a mile to the next notice board at Buttermilk Hill Spinney. Here you turn right on the public footpath track which comes up from Little Dalby.

N.B. If the permissive path is closed you will need to turn left and go downhill from the notice board. Go through the bridle gate and follow the bridleway across the field. It should be clearly visible even if the field is ploughed. Meet the Dalby road just to the right of Home Farm. Turn right and walk along the road towards Little Dalby.

The road bends sharp right at the Hall entrance gates, after a few more metres a footpath is signposted as the Jubilee Way. Turn right onto this which leads to the east end of the permissive path near the Punch Bowl Covert, where you rejoin the main Round route heading south to Somerby.

Both routes now continue into the Punch Bowl. Continue straight ahead to pass through a gate at the foot of steps (⊗ SK 77500 12310). Here a seat has been provided by the late Jim Mason for you to rest before climbing up to the top of the ridge. From the top there are fine views and the spire of Somerby can be seen ahead. Aim for a point slightly right of the spire and keep in this direction (due south). There should be a discernible line of footprints to show you the way across the dip of the second open field and up to a waymarked corner (⊗ SK 77530 11605). Walk with the hedge over to your right in the next field. When the hedge ends, continue in the same direction across the open field. Ahead of you lies a wooded hollow with a stream, crossed by a plank bridge (⊗ SK 77628 11200), then steps allow you to climb the bank. The next way marked stile leads you up into the corner of a field, close to the hedge on your left.

Move slightly right at the field corner to cross into a small corner of rough ground. Continue close to the hedge on your left in the next field. Cross the track which leads to the sewage treatment plant on your left and continue in the same direction between fencing which leads you into a jitty between houses on the main street of Somerby, opposite Manor Lane. Somerby church and village shop are to your left. The Stilton Cheese Inn is to your right.

SOMERBY, *is a beautiful ironstone village set in lovely parkland with horse pastures. Its most famous inhabitant was perhaps the dashing Fred Burnaby who is described as a 'thoroughly English type of man, robust, conservative, aristocratic soldier, opaque in intellect but indomitable in muscle'. He wrote a Victorian travel book called "The Ride to Khiva", and died fighting Arabs in the Sudan. There is a memorial window to him and his father, who was vicar, in the church. There is a shop and pub in the village. The village Memorial Hall is just that and marks the heroic efforts of the 10th Battalion, the Parachute Regiment dropped behind enemy lines in 1944. The village was shocked when only twenty eight survivors arrived back in Somerby to what was planned as a heroes return.*

© Crown copyright

SOMERBY - HALLATON

This section goes over high ground and through muddy wet woodland. Be prepared! Inspection of the OS map will offer a road alternative in severe conditions. If you need any provisions of food and drink, stock up at Somerby, as the route now crosses very thinly inhabited countryside.

From Somerby we go downhill, crossing various headwaters of streams which feed into the Wreake to the west and the Gwash to the east. In one of these little stream valleys we pass close to the site of the 12th century Owston Priory, and then go through the muddy Owston woods to reach Withcote and Launde. Near Launde we cross the border into Rutland. (Rutland was administratively part of Leicestershire for a short period when the original route was planned and launched.) This section goes beside the little river Chater and then up and over the Ridlington Ridge on farm tracks. There are spectacular views from the top of the ridge. The path then drops gently to Belton in Rutland. This is land that was once part of a Royal forest, established in the 12th century by Henry I. It was later released from royal control, gradually reduced in size and re-named the Leighfield Forest.

SOMERBY - LAUNDE ABBEY
(4 ½ miles)

From the main street in Somerby take Manor Lane. This is opposite where the last section ended. A gate at the end leads into a long, narrow field. Follow the bridleway uphill keeping close to the hedge on your right. Go through the gate to the right of the telegraph pole. The hedge is now on your left and cables overhead. The path joins a farm track and a stream appears on the left. When the field opens out to your left (⊗ SK 77768 09920) continue in the same direction to a gate. The hedge and stream return, now look for a wooden bridge over the stream. Cross the bridge and go up the bank. Turn right to walk with the stream down on your right. Go through the gateway ahead. You might be able to pick out the church spire at Tilton on the Hill ahead. Bear left to walk uphill with the hedge on your left.

At the next gate turn left around the side of the field where a seat in the corner (⊗ SK 77630 09032) offers a fine view south. Walk downhill close to the hedge on your left in this field and the next. The gate onto the road is just to the right of the bottom corner. Turn left and walk along the road into Owston. Ignore the road on the right to Marefield, Lowesby and Twyford, unless you wish to make a slight detour to see Owston church and the remains of the old abbey.

OWSTON *is now only a tiny hamlet but the humps and hollows in the fields show evidence that this was once a large Augustinian foundation. An engraving of 1730 reproduced in Nichols 'History and Antiquities of Leicestershire' published in 1795 shows the abbey and an impressive gatehouse which stood to the south west of the church. North of the Marefield road are the remains of fishponds.*

Pass the road to Knossington on your left and continue along Main Street which swings left to meet the Tilton road. Along the way note the old village pump on the right. 100 yards along the road turn right towards Tilton and Leicester.

Turn left nearly opposite the village sign into a green lane signposted 'Leicestershire Round' to Withcote. Continue along the lane to the very end, ignoring the path on the right to Wood End. A gate leads into a grassy field. Continue in the same direction, with a hedge on your left, but gradually bear right away from the hedge. Go through the waymarked gate (⊗ SK 78410 07335) at the top of the field, ignoring the gate in the corner of the field if you have stayed too close to the hedge.

From the gate, go to the gap in the bottom right corner of the field. Continue in the same direction moving uphill in a big field, parallel with the hedge over to your right. Go down the slope to

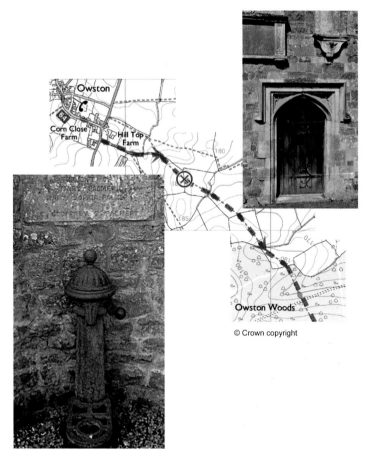

© Crown copyright

pass the corner of the wood on your right and then uphill in the same direction. You enter the wood via a hand gate alongside a metal field gate about 40 metres from the left edge of the wood.

At 141 acres Owston Wood is the largest area of ancient woodland in Leicestershire and has been a Site of Special Scientific Interest (SSSI) since 1956. It is managed by the Forestry Commission and is part of their 'Ancient Woodland Plan'. Consent has been given to stray a little from the muddy path but the wood is not open for public access.

The path through the woods is straight but usually wet and muddy. This short distance can be very wearisome, but the path emerges onto a beautiful avenue of chestnut trees which leads straight down to the Tilton-Oakham road. Cross with care and continue along the concrete farm road into Withcote.

WITHCOTE was one of the great houses visited by Leland conducting his survey for Henry VIII. He describes it as 'a right goodly house' but remarks that 'it standeth lowe and wet and hath a pole (pool) afore it'. You may find some of that wet ground near the pool sticks to your boots. It can still be very muddy. The owner of the house at the time of the Civil War (Smith of Withcote) took the wrong side when he supported the Parliamentary forces, and the lordship later went to the Crown. Withcote Chapel standing in the Hall grounds has lovely 15th century German glass. It is now in the care of The Churches Conservation Trust and is usually open and worth a look as the approach also offers a better view of the hall (bear right at the fork).

After the gate fork left and continue alongside a tall stone wall on your right. When the wall ends follow the track as it bends right between farm buildings to a metal hand gate. The rear of the Hall is now visible on the right and ahead is the pool. Walk close to fencing on your right and join a well-defined track close to the pool on your right.

Cross a bridleway then pass the barn on your left. Climb uphill, our path to Launde Abbey goes over the hill just to the right of the brow (⊗ SK 79712 05282) and down to a footbridge over the River Chater at the point where the telegraph wires cross the stream. (Aim for the road through Launde Park, climbing the hillside opposite until you spot the yellow topped post and gate).

Over the footbridge, cross the gulley then climb the steep bank. Turn right and head for Abbey Farm ahead but veer slightly left as you cross the big pasture to meet the road at a cattle grid in front of Launde Abbey.

© Crown copyright

LAUNDE ABBEY *This large and impressive Tudor house is beautifully situated in the bowl of the hills and among trees in a quiet secluded valley above the little river Chater. It was built for Thomas Cromwell on the site of the wealthy priory, founded in the reign of Henry I. Cromwell 'bagged' it for himself at the time of the Dissolution of the Monasteries, when he wrote in his private papers "Item to remember, myself for Launde". He did get possession, but only for three years, before he was executed in 1540. The name Launde suggests a clearing in the woods which once formed the Rutland forest. The house is now a Christian retreat and conference centre for the Leicester and Peterborough dioceses of the Church of England. It is usually open to casual visitors for coffee, lunch and tea.*

LAUNDE ABBEY - BELTON
(3 ½ miles)

From the cattle grid at Launde crossroads turn left along the road towards Withcote for a short distance and then turn right along the well-marked bridleway. Go through the gate and continue up the slope between the abbey, on your right and the lake on the left. Also on your left is the entrance to the Abbey's ice house.

The path leads you, parallel with a railing fence over to your right, towards the corner of Launde Park Wood. Go through the gate to the left of this corner then bear diagonally left across the big field to the far left corner and a gate. (If the path is obstructed by a crop. a headland has been left, for ease of walking, which follows the edge of Laude Park Wood).

Go through the gate ($\otimes$ SK 80940 04432) (to enter Rutland) and cross the bridge over the little River Chater. Follow the fenced bridleway, ignoring the signed bridle path off to the left.

At a crossing path, turn right along the wide yellow shale farm track. Follow this track, initially downhill bending right then left, to re-cross the Chater before climbing all the way up to the top of the hill (Y SK 80955 03195). From the top you can look left along the Ridlington Ridge and perhaps catch a glimpse of Rutland Water to the northeast. Where the track bends left, take the bridleway opposite and go down the hill. The track bends left to cross an open field with Eyebrook reservoir ahead in the far distance.

EYEBROOK RESERVOIR was created for Stewarts and Lloyds by damming the Eye Brook and was completed in 1940 to supply water to the Corby steel works. It is still privately owned and does not form part of the drinking water supply network.

Continue with the hedge first on your left then also on the right until you reach the road, near the big brick house, Brickle Farm.

Turn left along the road and walk for a mile into Belton. Chapel Street leads you to the memorial cross and the church. The Sun pub is a little further down the hill, on Main Street and is only open evenings.

BELTON in RUTLAND *is a pretty village with many attractive houses including a row of ironstone cottages with mullioned windows. It is so quiet and rural that it is surprising to find it close to the main A47 road and only 3 miles from Uppingham. Today it is a commuter village with good links to Peterborough and Leicester but the many grand old houses suggest this has been a country retreat for years. Between 1974 and 1997 Rutland was part of Leicestershire hence when the Leicestershire Round was created in 1987 it passed this way. During this period Belton's name was extended to distinguish it from Belton in northwest Leicestershire. On Godfrey's House a plaque, unveiled in 1982 by the Duke of Rutland, of Belvoir Castle in Leicestershire, commemorates the renaming. Many named walking routes converge here so take care to stay on the Leicestershire Round.*

BELTON - HALLATON
(4 miles)

Between Belton and Hallaton our route is also the Macmillan Way. From Belton church on Chapel Street walk downhill from the war memorial, along Nether Street and Littleworth Lane to reach the busy A47 Leicester-Uppingham road. Cross the road and continue along Allexton Lane, crossing the bridge over the Eye Brook and back into Leicestershire. The lane swings right. Ignore the road to Hallaton and continue along the 'No Through Road' towards Allexton Hall.

ALLEXTON *is a tiny village beside the Eye Brook, which forms the Leicestershire-Rutland frontier. It had a mill, recorded in Domesday Book, until 1912. The church of St. Peter is basically late Norman (1160-80) and the Hall, originally Elizabethan, was later converted to a farmhouse and partly taken down in 1843, then rebuilt in 1902. Allexton was the base of Hasculf de Hathelakeston, warden of the Forest of Rutland, who was given permission after the great storm of 1222 to dispose of fallen trees here. More recently when the village inn, the Wilson's Arms was sold by the brewery in 1968 a restrictive covenant was imposed to prohibit future sales of alcohol. The building is now Bridge House Farm.*

Pass Allexton church on your left. The gate to Allexton Hall lies ahead but ignore this instead turn left at the village green and go up the lane between houses to the end. A new house 'The Coppice' is on the left and the path appears to start through their

© Crown copyright

garden (this path used to be very muddy but now has a good stone surface). At the end of the track enter an open field and turn right to follow a bridleway. Allexton Hall parkland is hidden on your right. Just before the field ends turn left to walk uphill on a footpath to meet the hedge at a waymarked gate by a pole in the hedge (⊗ SK 81305 00005). Pass through the gate and cross big ploughed fields aiming for Allexton Lodge hidden behind trees on the hill ahead. At the trees turn right to follow the wire fencing on your left and turn uphill to pass Allexton Lodge.

Turn right at the first hedge past the house and walk downhill, close to the hedge on your left and with overhead wires above. Bear left to go through the gate and head for the corner of a fenced plantation. Here a seat offers views up the Welland valley (⊗ SP 80325 98972). From here you should see Fearn Farm, your next target, on top of the hill on the far side of the valley. The gate is just to the right of the farm barns. At the lane turn left to pass Fearn Farm on your left and turn right to go through the wide gate near some sheep pens. Keep close to the hedge on your right for two fields.

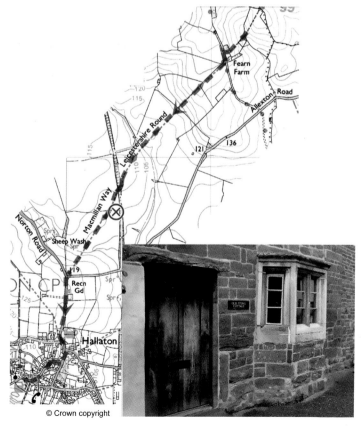

© Crown copyright

Cross the double stile and continue in the same direction downhill across the huge ploughed field (usually the path is well marked). In the dip cross the footbridge over the stream. Continue but swing left approaching the line of trees, to reach a bridge. This is over the long-disused Melton Mowbray - Market Harborough railway line. Cross the bridge and go down the slope. Continue in the same general direction across another large open field, passing the end of a hedge on your right (⊗ SP 79290 97637), to the top right corner. Meet the Hallaton Road at the junction with Allexton Road. Follow the road into Hallaton, passing the sports pavilion on your left. The Fox Inn lies just beyond the duck pond. From the inn wind your way down through the village to reach Hallaton church.

HALLATON *is one of Leicestershire's prettiest villages, famous for its Norman motte and bailey castle site, its fine church, market cross and the annual bottle kicking on Easter Mondays.*

It has two pubs and a cafe/deli where meals can be obtained, a duck pond, a village museum and a small lock up (no longer in use!). You really need to give yourself a breathing space here to take in the beauties of the village. It lies on the edge of the stone belt and has houses of brick and of stone. The oldest brick house is dated 1691. The green, which forms the centre of the village and is one of its most attractive features, is surrounded by old stone and thatch buildings. On it stands the Butter Cross, a conical stone structure with a circular base and a ball finial, probably dating from the late 17th century. Near it is the War Memorial given by Mrs Bewicke in 1921 in memory of her son. The 'Bewicke Arms', a mid-17th century stone building with a steeply-pitched thatch roof, is at the south-east corner of the green. On the green's north side is a much-restored thatched cottage, formerly the smithy, and behind it stands the Conduit House.

The Fox Inn at North End dates from the early 19th century. In Hog Lane, between High Street and Hunt's Lane, are six charity homes built in 1842, while on Horn Lane is the impressive village hall, Stenning Hall built in 1925 along with the Isabella Stenning charity houses of 1924 on High Street.

Dated tablets on buildings suggest that much modernisation was carried out by J.H.Dent in the mid-19th century. The village had a station on the railway from Melton Mowbray to Harborough but this was closed 1953. The village museum is now located by the church in the old tin tabernacle.

The stream just to the south of the village, flowing south-east, is the scene of the Hallaton bottle-kicking contest which takes place between the villages of Hallaton and Medbourne each Easter

Monday, after the formal cutting and distribution of a hare pie at the Rectory. Each village attempts to gain possession of one or both of the two wooden 'bottles' or casks, which are hooped with iron and filled with ale. Hallaton Hall stands on the east side of the village, near the junction of three roads, its grounds surrounded by a high wall. From 1713 until the middle of the 19th century it was the home of the Bewicke family. The castle site is one of the finest in the county. It stands just outside the village but can be seen from our route, if you remember to turn back for a birds eye view as you climb the hill towards Othorpe. The castle was a motte-and bailey construction, surrounded by a deep ditch. The motte is the mound and the bailey the outer yard. The purpose of the castle was to protect an iron-working site and signs of the iron working are visible in the valley.

In 2000 the largest hoard of British Iron Age coins was discovered here. Now known as The Hallaton Treasure, Harborough museum has some of the finds on display.

HALLATON - FOXTON

As you move south from Hallaton the ground becomes less hilly. You will walk, at Glooston, near the Gartree road, where Romans walked and built their villas. The route goes beside the willow lined stream to Stonton Wyville and over the Langton Caudle hill, with good views over the five villages which form the Langtons. The five Langton villages are strung out along the crest of a little range of hills between Kibworth and Welham. Church Langton is the 'capital', with its 'satellites' East, West, Thorpe and Tur Langton. The route does not pass through Tur Langton, but its tall red brick spire can be clearly seen. The church with its fancy brick patterning was designed by Joseph Goddard, who also designed the Leicester clock tower. After crossing the busy A6 road, you approach Foxton, and can refresh yourself at pubs in the village or press on to the tourist destination at Foxton Locks.

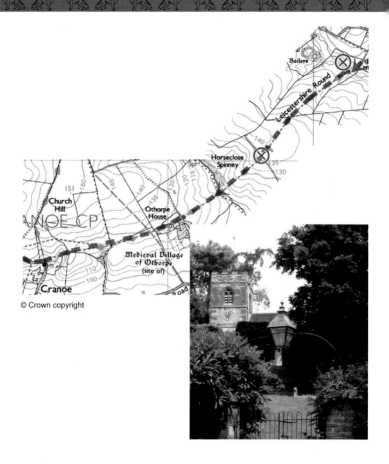

© Crown copyright

HALLATON - GLOOSTON
(3 miles)

From Hallaton church walk up Churchgate bending right then left past the school. At the top where the road ends, go straight ahead through the kissing gate to the right of the little cemetery. Walk close to the hedge on your left (ignore a stile in the fence) use the gate and keep straight on down the slope, to cross a ditch. Turn left, cross another stream (⊗ SP 78275 96590) then go up the hill moving slightly to your right. Continue uphill, moving further away from the hedge on the left towards the hedge on the skyline. Here two gates, located about 150 metres from the hedge on your left, allow access to the next field. Continue over the brow of the hill, keeping in the same direction. Pass close to a fenced enclosure with pond and trees on your left and go through the waymarked handgate to cross a drive to the farm on your right (⊗ SP 77645 96035).

From here, aim for Othorpe House at the top of the hill beyond the valley. Go downhill to cross the footbridge and continue uphill to the farm. Head to the right of the trees which surround the house, then cross the track. Othorpe House, to your left, is all that remains of the deserted Medieval village. Go between the barns, pass the redbrick barn on your left, and turn left and right behind a new barn on a narrow path at the top of a bank.

Cross the little paddock, close to the hedge on your right. Continue parallel with a hedge over to your right as you continue along the hillside. When the hedge begins to bend left cross through the gap and keep in the same direction with the hedge now a few yards on your left.

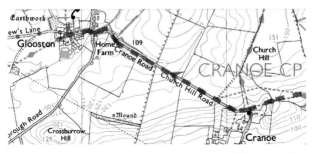

© Crown copyright

A path forks off right across the field, ignore this. Aim for the top left corner by pine trees where a gate leads to the next undulating field and keep straight on past the isolated telegraph pole. Pass Cranoe Old Rectory down to your left and go through the gate opposite the little church of St. Michael (usually well hidden in the trees). The tiny village of Cranoe lies down below the church by-passed by our route.

Turn right and walk for a mile along the road to Glooston. At the crossroads continue in the same direction to pass the Old Barn Inn on your left.

CRANOE has belonged to the Brudenell family of Deene (Northants.), subsequently Earls of Cardigan, since the 16th century. The church of St. Michael was severely damaged by a storm in 1846 and then rebuilt. The National School on the corner of School Lane is built of ironstone and carries the date 1843 with the arms of Lord Cardigan on the central gable. It was erected by the 7th Earl of Cardigan for children who walked to school from the four parishes where the Brudenell estates lay - Cranoe, Stonton Wyville, Glooston and Slawston. The Cardigan Arms public house is now a private house.

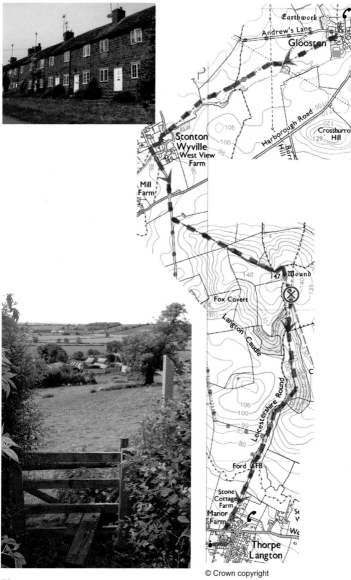

© Crown copyright

In the churchyard two impressive memorial obelisks mark the resting place of the McTurk family of Muirdrockit and Blaston. A cup bearing the family name is still awarded at the local sheep dog trials.

GLOOSTON is a small village near the Roman Road from Colchester to Leicester, a section between Huntingdon and Cambridge is now the busy A14. The Gartree Road, as it is now called in Leicestershire, is named after the Gore tree, an ancient thorn tree. Glooston church, rebuilt in 1866, dates back to 1220. If you go in the church you can see a sampler sewn in 1879 by a girl of 10.

GLOOSTON - THORPE LANGTON
(3 miles)

Continue with the Old Barn Inn on your left. Walk along the track between the church and the village hall. In the open field, aim for the pylon in front of you. Cross the stile to the right of the small water treatment works in the corner on your left.

In the next three fields the willow-lined stream winds its way over to your left while the path goes across the fields to Stonton Wyville. The waymarked crossing points are slightly to the right of the field corners. Meet the headland track into Stonton Wyville and continue past farm barns on your right. Follow the road round to the church at the T junction. Here a seat offers rest.

59

STONTON WYVILLE *In a shady churchyard, the modest little 13th century church of St. Denys makes an interesting and quiet stop. It was restored in 1863 by Goddard of Leicester, and has a 13th century font at which Robert de Wyville, who became Bishop of Salisbury in 1337, was baptised. The row of arches on the south side of the church show it was once, or was intended to be, much larger. In the chancel there is an Elizabethan high altar tomb to Edmund Brudenell. Various monuments to the Brudenell family remain. In 1628 Thomas Brudenell was created Baron Brudenell of Stonton and for many years the village was called Stonton Brudenell.*

The extensive fishponds beside the manor house date from the time when the village was a much larger and more important site. The former Fox and Hounds inn, opposite the church, is now a private house. In 1862 an inquest was held here after the boiler of a steam engine, being used to drive a threshing machine, exploded killing several villagers. Mill Farm is the former water mill, but the windmill which is marked on top of the Caudle, on Prior's map of 1777, has gone. The original route of the Leicestershire Round did not go over the Caudle. If you wish to avoid the climb continue along the field road.

At Stonton Wyville church turn left, cross the bridge and walk to the Kibworth-Cranoe road. Cross the road and follow the field road, signed 'Unsuitable for motors'. After 150M turn left at the bridleway sign (signposted to Welham) and go diagonally uphill across the field to reach the top left corner. After the gate bear left uphill with the hedge on your right and to the left open views back to Cranoe and Glooston. Ignore the wooden hand gate on the left and at the metal gate turn right. Follow the hedge on your right to reach the Triangulation Pillar at 147M above sea level, phew! Pause to take in the panoramic views.

Continue downhill from the trig point with the hedge on your right (the correct line of the path is in the centre of the field (Y SP 74573 94100) but is little used). Cross the stile at the foot of the hill and continue through the long sloping valley pasture to the spinney at the far end. Go through the spinney on a well-trodden path. Swing right to enter the next long pasture field and follow the tiny stream on your right. Go down to the ford, by the bottom right corner of the field.

Cross the footbridge beside the ford and continue up the track to Thorpe Langton, emerging by the Bakers Arms on your left.

THE LANGTONS *Church, Tur, Thorpe, East and West. Church Langton is the site of the early settlement but no longer centres one of the four civil parishes. Langton Caudle is in fact in Welham parish. The Reverend William Hanbury (1725-77) became vicar of Church Langton in 1753. His parishioners criticised him as a preacher for neglect of humble parish matters, rushing services and omitting prayers. The young man's interests really lay elsewhere. Hanbury a philanthropist and eccentric was a passionate botanist and market gardener. A Trust set up by him built the extensive school and school house at Church Langton in 1874, his grand plan to create a college complex here never materialised.*

St Leonard's church at Thorpe Langton was much restored by Joseph Goddard of Leicester in 1867 with £1,000 being provided by the Hanbury Trust. Having earlier been a chapel to the mother church at Church Langton there were no burials here until the middle of the 19th century.

THORPE LANGTON-
EAST LANGTON
(1 mile)

© Crown copyright

From the track by the Bakers Arms turn right along the road then first left along Church Lane. Turn right to pass the church on your left. Follow the walled green path which leads into an open field and continue to the redbrick house ahead, dated 1823 in brick patterning. Turn left here along the green lane then into the open field. Turn right to follow the hedge on your right.

To your left there are wide views across the Welland Valley. The route to East Langton is now almost due west. Follow the series of waymarked gates. As you approach the houses of East Langton note the large lake at Astley Grange to your left. Move slightly left to the field corner then right down a slope to enter the last little field. Go straight across this and then swing sharp left up a short length of old hedged way to a gate. Turn right along Back Lane then right again up the main street to reach The Bell Inn at a fork in the road.

EAST LANGTON *is a charming village, with a pub, idyllic cricket ground, and impressive former stables, these once offered local employment providing horses for the hunting field. The village was home to John William Logan a railway contractor (Logan and Hemingway). He came to The Grange in 1876 and stayed for the rest of his life. He was on two occasions Liberal MP for Harborough. He died in 1925 and is buried in the churchyard. Many features in the village are his work including the castellated water tower and cricket ground (beyond the Bell Inn). The Langtons were once served by a railway station (1857-1968) at East Langton just north of the narrow bridge on the B6047 Melton Road.*

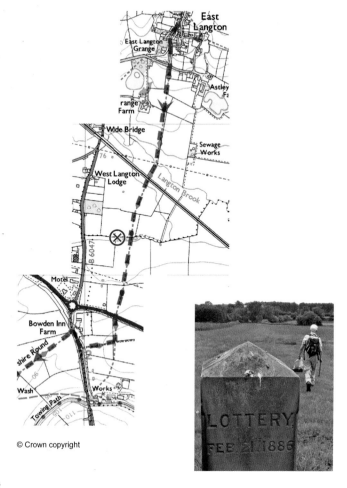

© Crown copyright

EAST LANGTON - FOXTON
(3 miles)

From the Bell Inn, East Langton, cross the road and turn left. Take the right fork in the main street and walk downhill between the imposing castellated tower of East Langton Grange and the converted stables, between high brick walls and under a magnificent copper beech tree. Continue down the leafy lane to the T-junction. Cross the stile opposite and note the factory in the distance, the route now heads for this going almost due south to the A6 Harborough by-pass. A series of gates and yellow topped posts offer an easy route across mainly pasture.

Pass close to the stone monument inscribed 'LOTTERY Feb. 21st 1886'. This we believe remembers a once famous racehorse that won the first Grand National in 1839. It spent time at Astley Grange Farm Stud close by.

Cross the footbridge over the Langton Brook and follow the hedge on your right to pass under the railway bridge (the main Leicester-St. Pancras line).

What is now the Midland Main Line was built by the Midland Railway in 1857 to provide its own route to London avoiding the LNWR via Rugby. Initially it linked from Bedford to the GNR at Hitchin before the opening of St. Pancras station in 1868.

Continue across two open fields towards a plantation including tall poplar trees (⊗ SP 72325 91253). Pass through the plantation and cross the bridge. Ahead of you, on the skyline, is the tall chimney of the factory which has been hidden since the start of the path. Marked on old maps as Gallows Hill Bone Mill, J.G. Pears still carry on an associated trade, animal rendering, which might explain the smell.

Walk towards it across the next two fields, going under the power lines. When you reach the busy A6 Market Harborough by-pass road use the steps and cross carefully. Continue in the same direction, close to the hedge on your right, for one field then turn right along a track towards the B6047 Harborough Road. Turn right and go uphill to the road. Turn right towards the big roundabout for a short distance, passing Bowden Business Village down to your right, and then cross the road carefully (a fast food outlet is located at the roundabout).

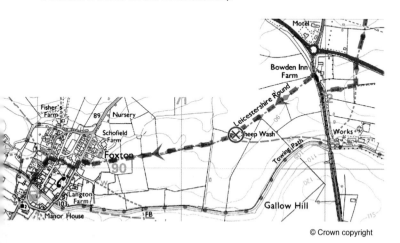

© Crown copyright

Go down the concrete slope and turn right through the gate into the corner of the field. Move slightly away from the hedge on your right, aiming for a point 100 metres from a dilapidated brick barn in the field corner. Continue across the next field and pass on your left the corner of a field which juts into this large field. Over to your left on the hill side a large hedge marks the level winding course of the canal arm between Market Harborough and Foxton. Cross the footbridge (⊗ SP 71375 90233) and go across the corner of the next field to cross a second footbridge. Continue walking close to the hedge on your left. Continue in the same direction but with the hedge now on your right. When it turns away from you, go downhill across the humpy field to cross the footbridge just to the left of some bungalows. Go uphill across the field to the far corner. A gate leads to a track between houses and onto Swingbridge Street in Foxton.

Turn left along Swingbridge Street passing Groooms Lodge, then turn right along a hedged footpath between houses, left again up Middle Street and right through another metalled footpath onto Main Street, opposite the Shoulder of Mutton pub (Texas Steakhouse). Turn left and walk up Main Street towards the church tower and the Black Horse pub. At the canal turn right along the towpath.

CANAL COUNTRY
(8 miles)

FOXTON - BRUNTINGTHORPE

In this section we start with easy towpath walking alongside the canal, passing the famous staircase locks, then across fields and uphill to Gumley. The way to Saddington is ups and downs, over the old gorse hill then down again to cross the reservoir streams but you are rewarded with marvellous views. Saddington village offers refreshment. The next few miles are not so hilly as you pass Fleckney. From here the route turns south to pass through the pretty village of Shearby before arriving at Bruntingthorpe having walked over slightly flatter land (but do not let anyone tell you that Leicestershire is flat!).

FOXTON - GUMLEY
(1 ½ miles)

FOXTON LOCKS - *The route continues along the towpath, if you wish to visit the Locks you will need to cross the pedestrian swing bridge, near The Foxton Locks Inn. A toilet block is immediately opposite the swing bridge and refreshments are available at either The Foxton Locks Inn or Bridge 61 opposite. The locks museum site makes an interesting stop.*

The first canal in Foxton was the Market Harborough Arm, from Leicester which opened in 1809. It was intended to continue to Northampton but money ran out. The steep staircase locks and twenty mile summit to Watford offered a link with the Birmingham to London canal. This route opened in 1814 but the locks became a bottleneck. In 1900 a boat lift was built to transport narrow boats quickly up or down the hill in a huge bath of water. There are museum facilities in the old Engine House, which explain how the system worked. It was a tremendous undertaking and expensive, taking three years to build, but it failed to attract new trade and was dismantled after only eleven years in use.

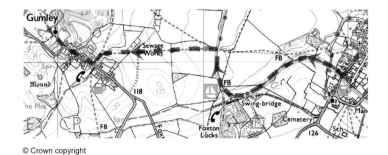

© Crown copyright

From Main Street in Foxton village (just below the Black Horse pub) turn right to walk along the towpath, with the canal on your left, to the basin at the foot of the Foxton Locks staircase. If you don't wish to explore, the Round continues swinging right to a high narrow footbridge (No.63). Turn left to cross the bridge and continue in the same direction, away from the canal and west towards Gumley. The church spire is just visible on the wooded hill ahead. Pass to the left of a small sewage treatment works, gates all the way. Don't be tempted by the track that climbs the hill in a narrow field, pass through the gate in a hedge of mature ash trees then bear left up the hill. Go through the passageway onto the Gumley village street. The Bell Inn lies to your left but you turn right to the church.

GUMLEY *is a pretty village, with its steep hills and dales and its cricket field and war memorial set in open parkland. It is easy to see that this was once an important site seated so imposingly on its wooded hill. The Scandinavian place name indicates an old settlement. There is a mound, a motte and the remains of an old hollow way in the fields south west of the village. The church was rebuilt in 1759 and the hall, which stood just south of the church, was built by Joseph Cradock in 1764. Cradock was a friend of Doctor Johnson and the actor David Garrick, and there was a private theatre which Garrick visited. Cradock spared no expense on the house but he had to sell it and live more modestly until he died aged 84. Hall Farm stable block built in 1870 with its Italian campanile tower, following the fashion set at Osbourne House built in 1845, is now all that remains. The hall was demolished in 1964. Masters of foxhounds and captains of cricket have lived in the village and kept the surrounding countryside attractive for their sport. The plantations of trees were designed by Reverend William Hanbury of Church Langton. By 1754 they were a local tourist attraction but the great gale of 1756 "blasted the tops of my elms and ash".*

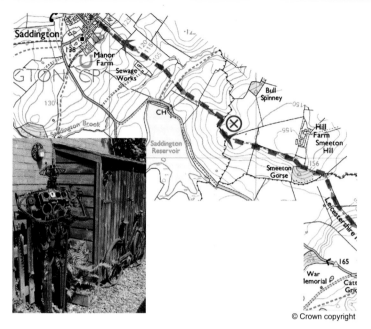

© Crown copyright

GUMLEY - SADDINGTON
(2 miles)

From Gumley, pass close to the church on your right and go through the spinney. Cross the open field, passing the magnificent copper beech, to the far corner.

Cross the road and walk close to the hedge on your right, downhill towards Smeeton Gorse hill and then uphill close to fencing on your left. From the top of the hill you have fine views all round and a seat from which to admire them. Smeeton Hill Farm lies over to your right. The path crosses the open corner of the field, near the gorse. Move slightly right to continue along the hillside, close to a hedge on your right.

When the hedge ends, keep in the same direction across the corner of a field then through a gap, here there is a view of Saddington Reservoir on your left. Follow the hedge on your left around the field with a little brick building in the middle of the field over to your right (⊗ SP 66770 91175). In the next field follow the hedge on your right then continue downhill to cross a series of footbridges.

The reservoir and dam, to your left, were built in the 1790's to feed the canal. The reservoir is fed by Laughton Brook. Our path crosses a number of channels which are:- the canal feeder, the original Laughton Brook used as an overflow, a feeder from the Saddington Brook (crossed twice) and finally the natural Saddington Brook.

Go straight uphill towards Saddington village. Cross the concrete cart bridge and move slightly left up the steep hill to reach a waymarked gate between trees. Go up the middle of this narrow field and join the enclosed path up the left side. This leads to Saddington village street. The church and Queens Head pub lie to your left.

SADDINGTON *During the summer, teas are served in the church which largely dates from 1872. The Queens Head pub serves food and there are views over the reservoir from the pub garden. Saddington Hall was the centre for Leicester Poor Boys and Girls Holiday Homes between 1927 and 1949. A new centre at Mablethorpe opened in 1936, offering a more appealing location for the children. The village also gives it name to a tunnel of 800 metres which transports canal boats under Kibworth Road on the edge of the parish.*

SADDINGTON - BRUNTINGTHORPE
(4 ½ miles)

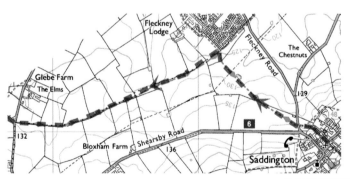

© Crown copyright

From our arrival point on Saddington Main Street take the lane opposite (Bakehouse Lane) passing Home Farm House on the left. Continue through the farm yard, joining the farm track which swings left to meet the Saddington-Fleckney road. Cross into the field on the opposite side of the road. Walk with the hedge on your right. When you are about halfway along, turn right through two gates and bear left making for a large pond with bushes round it in the middle of the field. Pass the pond on your right and go through the wide gap ahead. The village beyond is Fleckney. Continue as if towards Fleckney Lodge for a few yards only then turn sharp left in the middle of the field to join a bridleway. In the next field keep close to the hedge on your right then continue in this direction through a series of fields now with the hedge now on your left all the way to the road near Glebe Farm.

© Crown copyright

When you reach the road, go straight ahead along Fleckney Lane towards Arnesby for about 100 metres. After a farm entrance turn left onto the footpath, follow the hedge on your left for two fields. In the third field turn half right across the ridge and furrow heading towards farm buildings in the distance. You are seeking a hand gate near a big stone horse trough (⊗ SP 63253 91607).

From here continue in the same direction diagonally across fields. Cross a cart bridge over the stream and turn right (note the farm buildings ahead, seen earlier). Go gradually uphill to the top left corner of the field. Continue close to the hedge on your left, uphill towards New Inn Farm. Pass the farm on your right to meet the A5199 Welford Road. Turn left along the road then turn right along the road into Shearsby.

SHEARSBY *church stands on a high mound. Opposite is a very attractive timber framed thatched house with wattle and daub, dated 1669. There is a beautiful little pub, the Chandlers Arms. The village hosts an annual music festival on the green. There was once a mineral salt spring developed for a spa, which accounts for the Bath Spa Hotel, just outside the village.*

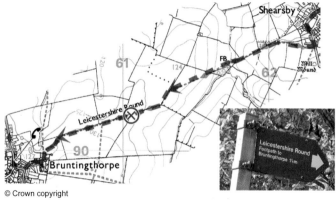

© Crown copyright

From Shearsby crossroads the church lies to your right, the village green lies straight ahead, and the Chandlers Arms lies to the left. Follow the road straight ahead round the village green and bend left along Back Lane into Mill Lane, signposted to Bruntingthorpe.

From Mill Lane, turn right into the field near the de-restriction sign. Walk close to the hedge beside the house on your right. Pass a pond on your left and continue with the hedge on your right. The path crosses into the adjacent field. Continue with the hedge now on your left. Move slightly right and down to cross the gated footbridge. Continue uphill, close to the fencing of a plantation of trees on your left, and keep in the same direction across a big field. This leads you onto a firm farm track beside a shed (⊗ SP 61050 90240). Follow the track when it swings left, past the old gravel pits on your left. At the cottages on Little End, turn right to join Main Street, Bruntingthorpe. The Plough Inn is on your left. Turn right towards Peatling Magna.

BRUNTINGTHORPE was an early settlement before the Anglo-Saxons came. The church dates from the 12th century. In Main Street there is a fine restored tithe barn of 1716. The airfield, constructed in 1942 for use of heavy bombers, is now a proving ground for the aviation, automotive and construction industries. An aviation museum on site is home to the Cold War Jet Collection. While not impinging on the Leicestershire Round the airfield does create a black hole into which many dead end footpaths links are lost.

BRUNTINGTHORPE - FROLESWORTH

As you walk along the first gentle stretch beside the small stream from Bruntingthorpe to Peatling Magna, you may see Arnesby windmill over to your right across the pasture fields. The path onward to Willoughby Waterleys is straightforward. It used to go absolutely straight, but we now make a slight kink at Mere Road, the old green lane separating the parishes. Willoughby is not, of course, waterless. It has streams on each side, with good pasture for cattle in the 'leys' - meadowlands. We now approach the M1 motorway which has cut across our route. The noise is very noticeable after the peace and quiet of our way so far! The old disused railway runs beside the motorway, a visible sign of how ephemeral our transport systems might be! Feet, created before trains or motor cars, take us to Dunton Bassett, from where we have a streamside walk to Stemborough Mill and then on beside a quiet lane to Leire. In Leire we cross another defunct railway line before a section of road walking to reach Frolesworth.

BRUNTINGTHORPE - PEATLING MAGNA
(2 miles)

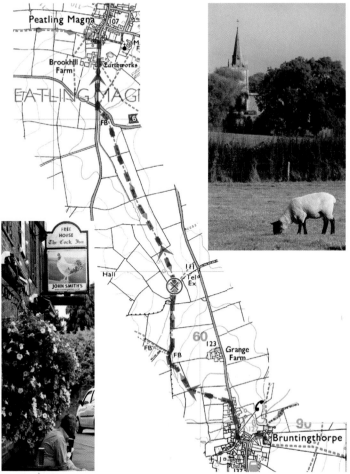

From Bruntingthorpe follow the road towards Peatling Magna. Turn left at the footpath sign by the last house (Apple Tree Cottage). Cross the field moving to your right, away from the house. Cross the fence, about 40 metres from the field corner. Continue in the same direction across a field corner. Bear right in the third field with a hedge on your right. Gradually move away from the hedge down to a gate near a stream hidden in a dense hedge. Keep close to the hedge and stream on your left for three fields. Note the building on your right by the road, a telephone exchange (⊗ SP 59833 90912). Ignore the path right up to the road. Our path continues but should now be across open fields about 50 metres from the stream. As you approach the road, move to the far left point of the last field, crossing the cart bridge to emerge at the crossroads junction. Follow the road uphill into Peatling Magna. The church lies in the field over to your right. As you enter the village turn left at Postal Cottage, opposite Holly Tree Farm. The Cock Inn can be found further along the road in the centre of the village.

PEATLING MAGNA is believed to have been settled in Roman times. It was a very early Saxon settlement with extensive earthworks to the east of the church. The 12th century church has tombs of the Jervis family, lords of the manor. The Manor House stands close to the church.

PEATLING MAGNA - WILLOUGHBY WATERLEYS
(1 mile)

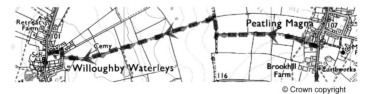

© Crown copyright

Follow the drive of Postal Cottage into the open field and cross to the right hand corner. Follow the hedge on your right to meet the old boundary, a hedged track (Mere Lane). Turn right along the track for 100 metres before turning left to follow the hedge on your right. Follow this all the way to Willoughby Waterleys, going gradually downhill to cross the stream, and then up to the village. When the houses come into view you need to cross the hedge to join a track. Follow the drive away from the cemetery and turn right along the lane. When this bends right, take the gate into the churchyard. Follow the path, passing the church on your left to arrive on the main street.

WILLOUGHBY WATERLEYS *is often spelt Waterless, most inappropriately considering its many springs and rivulets. The church is Norman, and the lovely Queen Anne house, The Limes, dates from 1702. The Old Hall is dated 1600 in blue brick, and Manor Farm is impressive. The Inn is named after George Augustus Eliott (1717-1790). He was the victorious Governor of Gibraltar during the Great Siege 1779-83. There are a number of inns across the country which honour his name even though he had no link with the location. The village hall was formally the school, built in 1846.*

75

WILLOUGHBY WATERLEYS - DUNTON BASSETT

(2 ½ miles)

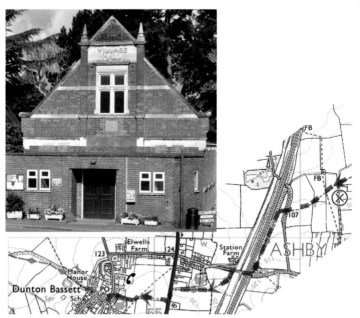

© Crown copyright

From Willoughby Waterleys church cross the road and pass the General Elliot pub on your right. Pass Orchard Road and after the terrace row turn right at the footpath sign. Follow the enclosed path into the open field then turn half left to go up the slope. Cross the stile then go through the gateway into the corner of the field, with a hedge and stream over to your right. Move to the far right corner of this field and continue with the hedge and stream on your right until you reach the road.

Turn right, pass the end of Broughton Lane on your right and continue along the main Ashby-Willoughby road for about 400 metres. Turn right at the footpath sign and keep roughly parallel with the hedge over to your right. In the next field, pass between the two lakes of Holy Farm Fishery. Locate a stile to exit the site, keeping in this direction across the next large field to reach a gate and stile onto the green lane which leads into Ashby Magna, on your left (⊗ SP 56258 91357).

Cross this lane and keep in the same direction, crossing to the far left corner of the second field. Continue in the same direction to meet a road. Cross the road and make for the motorway. Turn

left and walk close to the M1 motorway on your right for one long field. Pass the small brick hut on your left and go up the steps.

Turn right to cross over the motorway. Continue to the bridge over the disused Great Central railway and turn sharp left to descend the steep steps. Swing right to cut across the triangular field and in the next field walk close to the hedge on your right.

Meet the main A426 Lutterworth Road and turn left. Cross the road carefully to the footpath sign opposite the big garage (currently a car wash site) and walk with the hedge on your left for 200 metres until you are about two thirds of the way along the field. Cross into the corner of the little field on your left and turn right, to follow the same hedge, now on your right. The church is over to your left. Cross the next little hummocky field and follow the jitty path onto Main Street, Dunton Bassett.

The spire of **DUNTON BASSETT** *church lies ahead. The field near the 13th century church shows extensive signs of previous habitation. In about 1200 Geva, the lady of the manor, began the church building. There is a stone carving of her above the south vestry door. Her daughter Maud married a Sir Richard Bassett, which gives the village its present name. The school was endowed in 1849 by Mr Thomas Stokes, lord of the Manor of Dunton and a wealthy hosier of Leicester. There are at least two pubs in the village. The Post Office is also a general store. The Railway Hotel and Station Farm still stand on Station Road although the railway company named the station Ashby Magna.*

DUNTON BASSETT - FROLESWORTH

(3 ½ miles)

Turn left opposite the post office and follow the road to the right signposted to Leire and Frolesworth. Pass the Dunton Bassett Arms on your left and continue downhill along the No Through Road, passing the village hall on your left. You are now on the bridle road to Stemborough Mill. Follow the blue bridleway signs, ignoring the footpath off to the right. Pass a pond on your left and keep close to the hedge on your right until you cross the cart bridge (⊗ SP 54010 90887), where you swing left to keep close to the stream. Cross the open corner of the field and continue with the hedge on your left. Keep the stream on your left and pass the fishponds. Pass Stemborough Mill and swing left at Valley View Farm to follow the lane towards Leire. The original route followed this quiet lane but we now take the footpath right, under the cables, through the gate. Go diagonally across the field to the far corner. Pass a barn on your left. Cross the stile into the next field and follow the hedge on your left. In the next long field head for the far right corner where a stile takes you back onto the lane. Turn left along lane for 150 metres then right along a footpath over a series of stiles. The path then finally swings right to meet Main Street at Eaglesfield.

© Crown copyright

LEIRE has two nearby water mills, Stemborough Mill and Leire Mill, and two Inns, the Queens Arms and Crab and Cow (formerly the White Horse). There is a 17th century manor house and a Glebe House, built in 1793. The Church of St. Peter has its first recorded rector in 1210 (William de Leire). There is a shallow moat behind Airedale Farm although there is now no sign on the ground. Roman pottery and medieval paving have been found near the church. Part of the old railway line cutting has been bought by parishioners and donated as a popular Nature Walk which leads into Ullesthorpe. Leire had a station halt which opened in 1925 although the line had been in use since 1840, the first route from Leicester to London.

Leire church and the Queens Arms are to your left. Cross Main Street and take Back Lane leading to Wales Orchards. Pass the Crab and Cow, on the right, then Wales Orchard on your left and continue on the track 'unsuitable for heavy goods vehicles'. This is still Back lane which turns right. Here take the surfaced path linking to another road. Keep in the same direction. Pass Hoke Court on your left and when the road bends left follow the track ahead. This was Station Lane. Stiles allow access across the old railway line (⊗ SP 52198 90180), now the village nature reserve.

Continue up the next field initially parallel with the hedge over to your left then across the open field to the far hedge. Cross the stile and continue across the next field to the corner of hedge

Cross the next stile in the corner of the field, beside a telegraph pole. Move gradually left towards Hillcrest Farm on the hill. Turn right and walk along the road towards Frolesworth for a mile.

Go straight over the crossroads, passing the old almshouses on the corner where the Plough and Harrow pub once stood, to reach Frolesworth church.

FROLESWORTH *church has several small 15th century figures and 16th century alabaster monuments to the Staresmore family. Frolesworth House, opposite the church, has very impressive 18th century gates and gateposts. The almshouses date from about 1725 until 1824. The Plough and Harrow was demolished in 2002 and the site used for housing. The Dutch Barn at Manor Farm is a modern commercial office building but from a distance resembles a Dutch barn stacked with straw bale. This is best seen at a distance along footpath V32 from Sharnford.*

FROLESWORTH to BARWELL

From Frolesworth to Barwell the ground gently undulates offering some fine views along with level walking. We pass Claybrooke Mill and the fringes of Claybrooke Magna and Claybrooke Parva. Allow extra time if you wish to explore these villages. From Claybrooke it may seem rather a drag across big fields, but our destination is High Cross the centre of Roman England and as the name suggests the highest point on this section of the walk. There is a camp site and B&B at Victoria Farm. Our route from High Cross is along the pleasant and easy Fosse Way green lane. Sharnford sits in the upper reaches of the Soar and we approach through Fosse Meadows Country Park. The village provides some services. Before the M69 severed a number of footpaths our route could have passed through the pretty village of Aston Flamville. We now bypass the settlement sharing a road crossing. The direct line from here would lead to the village of Burbage but we turn away from the village. You may wish to make a detour to visit this attractive settlement. To avoid the Hinckley conurbation we take a popular route skirting Burbage Wood and across the Common. The final approach into Barwell has been changed to offer a safe crossing of the A47.

FROLESWORTH - CLAY-BROOKE PARVA

(2 miles)

© Crown copyright

Pass Frolesworth church on your left and continue along the road towards Sharnford. Turn left opposite White Cottage. Follow a track between houses. Initially walk close to the hedge on your left. Aim for Hill Farm beside trees on the hill ahead then continue gently downhill across the open field, moving away from the hedge on your left. Cross the waymarked footbridge and continue uphill to reach the farm drive to the left of the farmhouse. Pause to admire the views from this high point.

Continue downhill in the same direction, towards a mass of farm buildings (Claybrooke Grange). In the dip turn right and follow a small stream on your left across a sloping field to a gate/footbridge.

Cross the bridge and turn right following the stream now on your right. In the next field bear left and follow the hedge on the left. Claybrooke Magna is ahead to your right. Meet and cross Frolesworth Lane and keep in the same direction across the big open field to meet a bridleway at a metal gate. Join the bridleway to cross the wooden cart bridge over the mill race. Pass between modern sheds.

You have arrived at Claybrooke Mill. The building dates from 1675 but there was a mill marked on this site in the Domesday Book.

The old brick mill is to your right. Cross another wooden bridge over the stream. The bridleway forks off left. Keep to the footpath in the same direction, crossing the open field, parallel with a hedge over to your right and making for a point about halfway along the hedge ahead.

Claybrooke Magna sits on the hill in front of you. Continue up the long pasture field to a gate in the top left corner, this leads into Bell Street.

CLAYBROOKE MAGNA *has no church but it does have a very popular pub, The Pig in Muck, standing at the far end of the street. There are several houses with large barred windows which indicate that they were once frame knitters' cottages. The village is home to Whitmore's Timber yard, a large site but mostly hidden from view.*

About a third of the way along Bell Street turn left on the footpath to Claybrooke Parva. Well used by local churchgoers, it begins as a drive beside houses. This is usually a well kept and well walked route over two fields. Keep the hedge on your left. Claybrooke Hall is over to your left as you approach the road, while on your right admire a magnificent Sweet Chestnut tree with its twisting bark.

CLAYBROOKE PARVA *has a large and impressive church. Make a detour left along the road to visit. The chancel, which was built about a hundred years after the rest of the church, dates from 1340 and is particularly high, wide and light. The extensive green lawns under the imposing large trees make this a quiet resting place. The seats are good for picnic stops.*

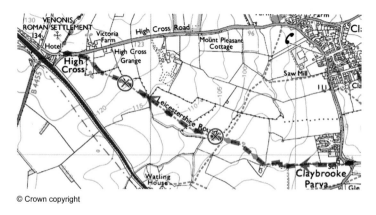

CLAYBROOKE PARVA - HIGH CROSS
(1 ½ miles)

At the road turn right ignoring the road to Monks Kirby and Brinklow on your left. As the road bends right turn left in front of the school to take the field edge path with the school hidden behind the hedge on your right. After about 200 metres the path veers to the right and goes through the hedge to the other side, continue with the hedge on your left to pass an isolated converted barn.

Pass through the gate. From here the path crosses the field but you may need to follow the left-hand hedge. When you get to the corner of the hedge, you should walk diagonally right across the field ahead of you. (The cross field paths to High Cross can be difficult with waymark posts hidden in hedges and walkers being left to make a path through the crops, so take care.) Go downhill to cross the footbridge (Y SP 48453 88120) then walk uphill, slightly away from the hedge over to your left. Continue across another large field and pass a protruding field corner on your right (Y SP 47820 88463). Victoria Farm is now in front of you, cross a grass field and go diagonally left into a narrow sharp corner of the field. Turn left at the road and walk to High Cross.

HIGH CROSS, *at the junction of two important Roman Roads was the centre of Roman England. The Fosse Way, (Lincoln to Exeter) and Watling Street, (Dover to Wroxeter near Shrewsbury), met here. The 4th Earl of Denbigh of Monks Kirby Warwickshire (1668-1717), was also Lord Lieutenant of Leicestershire. He caused the monument to be set up here in 1712 "as perpetual remembrance of peace at last restored". Only the base remains and this is very weathered so a transcript and translation of the Latin inscription is essential. It reads: "If, Traveller, you seek for the footsteps of the ancient Romans, here you may behold them. For here their most celebrated ways, crossing each other, extend to the utmost boundaries of Britain". A contemporary drawing shows the monument in open countryside three times the height of the base that we see today. Our route takes the quiet Fosse Way, but to see the monument continue along Bumblebee Lane to where it stands on the left.*

HIGH CROSS - SHARNFORD
(2 ½ miles)

Opposite the name sign 'Bumblebee Lane' take the track on the right protected by a white metal barrier. This is the old Fosse Way and previously this stretch could be quite muddy. The drainage has been improved and extensive sections have been surfaced with loose stones making it now an easy walk of a mile and a half.

When the surface changes to tarmac take the stile left into a pasture field opposite the gate to Claybrooke Lodge. Move diagonally left to the bottom left corner of the field and cross the access drive to Cottage Farm. Continue close to the stream on your left. Cross the footbridge and continue in the same

© Crown copyright

direction, moving away from the stream and hedge on your right. Cross another stream to enter Fosse Meadows and turn left. Cross a cart bridge and turn right at a T junction. This takes you around a lake and past observation hides on your right. At a crossing path dog leg right and continue, it is signed 'arboretum' (⊗ SP 48683 90957). Open space to your left may soon be planted with trees. A hedge comes in from the right follow this to the boundary of the reserve where a gate leads to a fenced path. Follow the fenced path passing the cricket field on your left. Cross the solid concrete bridge then follow the Soar Brook. Meet the road, with the Sharnford Arms pub and village store over to your right. Turn left onto the old road still alongside the brook then left onto Sharnford's main road. The Bricklayers pub lies ahead.

SHARNFORD *lies on the River Soar, near the Roman Fosse Way. It has been an important stopping place in times gone by. The 12th century church of St. Helens was damaged by fire in 1984 and then lovingly restored. Fosse Meadows was a commercial farm until purchased by Blaby District Council in 1987 for public recreation. The lake was created in 2002 and to date 49,000 trees have been planted creating diverse habitants across the 142 acre site.*

SHARNFORD - BURBAGE
(3 miles)

Pass The Countryman pub over to your left and continue straight ahead (on the right hand pavement of the One Way triangle).

Turn right along Aston Lane, in front of Roadley House Farm keeping the old redbrick farm buildings on your left. As the road bends right go over a stile under an oak tree and through the small paddock. Keep close to the fencing on your right. Keep in the same direction then bear right through the gap to cross the cart bridge over the Soar Brook. Pass the big modern sheds and continue close to the hedge on your right. Look for a gate in the hedge. Pass through this then bear left to follow the same hedge.

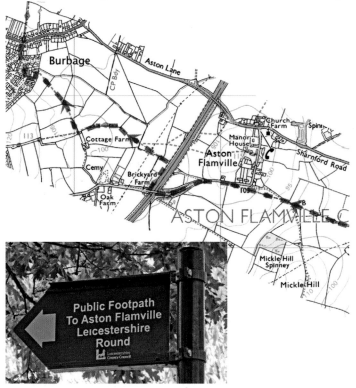

When the hedge bears left continue along a track across the field. Cross a ditch board (⊗ SP 47108 92037) into the next field and follow the hedge on the left. Pass under overhead cables and in the next field follow a hedge on right. A gate leads into pasture walk across the centre of the field. Cross two streams through twin gates and turn right to walk in the field alongside a track. Stay in the field when the track joins the road and finally join the road using a gate in the far corner. We have passed to the south of Aston Flamville.

ASTON FLAMVILLE *is only a hamlet but it has an impressive and charming church in a shady churchyard. One small window is Norman and there is a 16th century tomb to Sir William Turvil, his wife and their five children. There is also a little alabaster figure in Cromwellian armour. There is a fine 18th century manor house and, on the opposite side of the road in the field beside the church there is a great square dovecote dated 1715. It is worth the slight detour if you are in a mood to take photographs, but there is no public access to it.*

Aston Flamville

© Crown copyright

Join the lane on your right, from Aston Flamville and continue on the road towards Burbage (Lychgate Lane). Cross the motorway bridge and immediately turn right down the steps. Walk close to the motorway along an enclosed path then turn left towards a big pylon in the next field. Cross the stiles and footbridge in the field corner and pass the pylon on your right. Walk with the hedge on your left, the stile is a few metres from the corner. Cross the centre of the next field to a protruding corner. Cross into the next field and follow the hedge on your left. The spire of Burbage church is now visible among the trees. Cottage Farm, the redbrick house, is one field away to your left. Cross the stile into a scrubby field.

Our route to Burbage Common avoids BURBAGE a pleasant village and worth a visit. You might like to plan starting or ending a walk here where a series of blue plaques and information boards guide you through the village heritage. The path ahead leads straight into Aston Lane, Burbage should you wish to visit.

Our route turns right after crossing the stile with Burbage church spire over to your left. Walk close to the hedge on your right, cross the stile in the corner and continue in the same direction across the open pasture fields to reach a stile onto the housing estate road.

© Crown copyright

Turn left along Sherborne Road which bends right to join Salisbury Road, turn right past Dorchester Road to join Winchester Drive, turning right again to Sapcote Road (B4669).

BURBAGE – BARWELL
(2 ½ miles)

Cross the main Hinckley-Sapcote road and go through a gap between bungalows (Nos. 97 and 99) along a gravel path through a waymarked hand gate into a field with a hedge on your left. Half way along this very long field go through a gate in the hedge and continue in the same direction, but with the hedge now on your right. You are approaching Burbage Wood and Common, a popular area with lots of paths. Care is needed as the Round is not well marked across the Common

Go through three large fields, along the edge of Burbage Wood on your right. Cross a plank bridge into the open field at the end of the wood. Walk in the same direction, with the hedge now on your left. Wood House Farm, a.k.a. May's Café, over to your left, serves teas to thirsty walkers. Continue under the railway bridge.

BURBAGE COMMON *is the finest common in the county, 200 acres managed by Hinckley and Bosworth Borough Council. It is designated 'Access Land' by The Countryside and Rights of Way Act 2000 (CROW Act). The open area crossed by our route is being managed as a wildflower meadow.*

Across the common the route has been amended to offer easier navigation and refreshment. Take the centre fork signed to the Visitor Centre and Play Area. This crosses the open common along a bridleway, marked by blue topped posts, to the main car park and Acorns Coffee Shop. Turn left here passing the play area and follow the winding hedgerow over to your right. Enter the golf course to locate a yellow topped post by an information board (⊗ SP 44428 95205). Here a stile leads to an enclosed path. Follow this to the main road.

Cross the B4668 Hinckley to Leicester road and go down into the garden ahead. Keep close to the hedge on your right. Cross the stile and ditch and then walk with the hedge on your left before crossing the field to locate a gap to the right of the white cottage ahead of you.

The route from here has been amended into Barwell.

Turn right along Barwell Lane, a metalled cycle track. This bends left then drops down to pass under the A47. Two footpaths go off to the right, the first was unsigned at the time of writing but passes through a large gap in the hedge, ignore this. Our route is a few metres further on through a gate which hides under a tree. Walk across the field with the hedge a few metres to your right. In the far corner gates lead to the next field. Turn left up the field edge to Church Lane and Barwell church.

BARWELL *has long been known as a centre for the shoe industry, rather than for its charm or its history, but it was a settlement before the Romans came and Bronze Age fragments have been found here. There are a variety of shops and eating places here just 500 metres along High Street if you turn right.*

Turn left along Church Lane then left again into High Street which becomes Mill Street at the Red Lion. Continue another 200 metres then turn right into Moat Way.

BARWELL - SHACKERSTONE

From Barwell this section goes along the higher ground between the little River Tweed and Rogues Lane. We head towards Stoke Golding but turn north before reaching the village. Through the flatter landscape flows the Ashby Canal and we follow its towpath to reach Sutton Wharf, the entry to Bosworth Field battle site. You might like to allow extra time to visit the battlefield centre and the museum. You could perhaps watch the film with Sir Laurence Olivier playing Richard III. Sutton Cheney makes an interesting stopping point, both for its historical associations and for eating establishments. The next stop is the pretty market town of Bosworth (buses to Leicester) then just a few miles further on to Shackerstone. Here a restored Victorian railway and canal, both used purely for pleasure now add interest to our walk. There are frequent refreshments stops on the second half of this section.

BARWELL - SUTTON WHARF
(3 ½ miles)

NOTE there are plans to develop the land east of the A447 at Barwell (⊗ SP 43602 96665). We hope that a more attractive walking route will be provided but at the time of writing there are no details. Please check for updates before setting out.

From opposite No. 43 Mill Street, Barwell, turn into Moat Way and walk through the industrial estate. At the T-junction turn left to the end of the estate road and cross the small area of rough ground leading down to a plank footbridge over a stream. Walk close to the right hand hedge (which swings to the right) in this very long field and go through the gate. At this point you are level

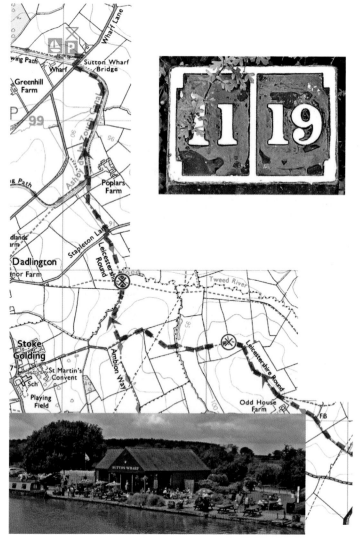

with Barwell House, the large redbrick building on your left and Bosworth House farm is ahead of you. Go diagonally left across this pleasant ridge and furrow field to locate a stile in the far corner onto the A447 Hinckley - Ashby road. This is a busy road so take care. Turn left along the verge for a few metres then cross to the footpath on your right to continue in the same direction. Walk with the hedge on your left through three fields. When the hedge bends right cross the substantial footbridge on your left. You now need to cross a huge field to reach Odd House Farm on the hill ahead. Aim for the right hand side of the house to join the farm track by a pond. Continue with the hedge on your right at first. At the next gap you will have the hedge on your left.

From the end of this field go diagonally left across the field to the end of a hedge (⊗ SP 42160 97517) then bear left again walking parallel to the hedge over to your left. Go through the gate in the hedge opposite and continue to the corner of the field which juts out. Keep the hedge on your left but move slightly right to reach the footbridge across the stream, about 20 metres from the corner.

The next field is big and open, with power lines crossing it. Move towards the right hand corner, crossing under the power lines. Go through the gateway and turn left along a farm track, Stoke Golding lies ahead. Look for a gate in the hedge on your left which indicates a crossing path. Turn right here across the field. Cross a stile and turn right to follow the winding hedge which hides a stream on your left. Follow this until you get close to the spinney. Cross the stream by the footbridge (⊗ SP 41417 97925). Walk with the stream on your right, officially the path goes across the field but the walked path stays close to the stream. Cross Stapleton Lane and the bridge then keep in the same direction with the stream now on your left. Follow the hedge on your right until you are about two thirds of the way along the field. Pass through the gate on your right and continue through the corner of the field. Go through gates and a ditch crossing to cross another small field and up to the canal bridge. The building over to your right is Poplars Farm. Cross the canal bridge, turn immediately left and descend the short, steep slope to the towpath.

This is the Ashby canal opened in 1804 to carry minerals found in Ashby Wolds around Moira. The canal never reached Ashby terminating at Overseal, here many tramroads linked the mines to wharves. It joins the Coventry canal near Bedworth and the twenty-two lock free miles make it restful boating for today's pleasure craft.

Turn left again to pass under bridge No. 33. Walk along the towpath with the canal on your right, go under the next bridge at Sutton Wharf. Climb the steps to your left and cross over the bridge. The road leads to Sutton Cheney village. Turn left into Sutton Wharf car park.

Sutton Wharf is a big basin for canal boats. There are toilets, café and information for Bosworth Battlefield. The battle fought near here in 1485 brought Henry VII to the throne when he defeated Richard III. A car park offers opportunity to walk a short section of the Round from here.

SUTTON WHARF - SUTTON CHENEY

(2 miles)

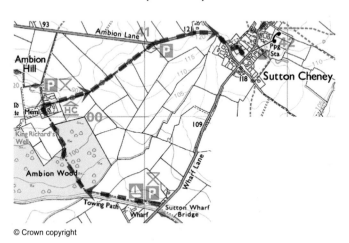

From the car park at Sutton Wharf follow the footpath on the north of the canal. The route is well maintained and leads to the Battlefield Centre. It begins by following the canal on your left and then enters Ambion Wood. A wide track leads through the trees, swings right and emerges in an open field with Ambion Hill Farm, the Battlefield Visitor Centre, immediately ahead. The centre is worth a stop, for its shop, museum, tea place and toilets.

Your route continues past the centre entrance on your right, and then turns sharp right along another well marked route, which goes straight beside a hedge on your left.

From the high ground here you may see the spire of Market Bosworth church in the wooded area to your left, and the little capped tower of Sutton Cheney church in front of you, slightly to your right.

The path meets the road short of the village but a roadside footway offers a safe walk along Ambion Lane. Swing right at the junction with Bosworth Road. As you enter the village a footpath sign points left. Take this but immediately bear right up a slope beside the little house then through a hand gate to enter the churchyard. Continue through the churchyard to reach the road passing the alms-houses hidden behind the church.

SUTTON CHENEY *is usually bedecked with beautiful flowers outside the cottages on the village street. The church of St. James is known locally as 'The Battlefield Church' and there is an old wooden sign bearing these words in the garden opposite the church. It is generally believed that Richard III celebrated Mass here the night before the Battle of Bosworth Field in 1485. Inside the church there are many items referring to Richard III including several needle point kneelers provided by members of the Richard III Society. An impressive row of 17th century alms houses stands beside the church. There is a fine manor house farm and two pubs.*

SUTTON CHENEY - MARKET BOSWORTH

(2 miles)

From the lychgate turn left past the Hercules Revived pub, the telephone box and the impressive Old Hall to reach the Royal Arms Hotel near the end of the village. Take the path left through the hotel car park. Bear left to a gate at the far side. Continue straight ahead across the field. Go through the gap in the hedge then turn sharp right. Walk with the hedge on your right and go through the gap to meet the farm track, which goes left, down

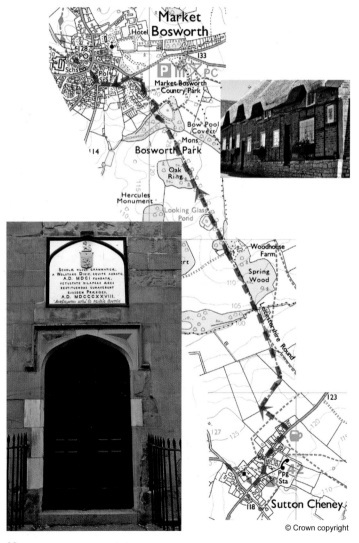

© Crown copyright

and round the edge of the field. The footpath goes diagonally left across the field corner, aiming for the house ahead in Spring Wood. Keep close to the hedge on your left to reach the brick bridge over the stream.

Now walk uphill, with Spring Wood on your right, to the isolated mock-Tudor farmhouse, Woodhouse Farm, at the edge of the wood. Cross the track and continue straight ahead through the clearing in the woods to join the avenue of trees which leads to Bosworth Park. Pass Looking Glass Pond and Oak Ring Wood on your left and then go through the hand gate into Market Bosworth Park and arboretum.

Cross a grass area with memorial benches then follow the stone paths through the park. Turn right at the crossing path to reach the corner of Bow Pool. Turn left passing the Country Park Ranger's hut on your left and continue to meet Rectory Lane. Follow Rectory Lane to the end turning right onto Sutton Lane to enter Market Place.

MARKET BOSWORTH *would make a good stopping point as it has shops, pubs, tea rooms, toilets, a market and a reasonable bus service. It usually provides a marvellous display of flowers for the Leicestershire in Bloom competition. The grammar school was founded in early Tudor times and funded by Sir Wolstan Dixie. Samuel Johnson was an usher (assistant teacher) here for a few months before he relinquished the job out of boredom and dislike of his treatment by the tyrannous Sir Wolstan Dixie to whom he was in service. The fine house on the square was built by the Dixies in about 1700. The 15th century church stands at the end of a pretty street. Towards the end of the 19th century the Dixie family had to sell the hall and parkland. From 1936 to 1988 the grand Queen Anne building, in red brick with white stone dressings, became a hospital. It is now a hotel. The former parkland is managed as a country park by Leicestershire County Council. Many living ramblers remember it as the site of a 20th century 'Battle of Bosworth' when the last Sir Wolston Dixie used to set up obstacles to prevent walkers crossing his land!*

MARKET BOSWORTH - SHACKERSTONE

(3½ miles)

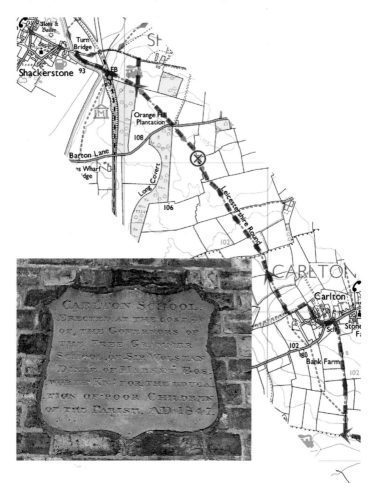

From Market Bosworth market place cross Main Street. Pass to the right of the old Dixie grammar school taking Back Lane between the impressive old bank and the Co-Op. Pass the public toilets on your right and continue downhill. When the road bends left take the track ahead then cross the stile right to walk downhill on a grassy enclosed track. Cross a few stiles and finally enter open countryside swinging gradually right to skirt a grassy mound on your right. Head towards houses on the edge of the town to meet a green lane and turn left. The lane becomes a farm track and then continues in the same direction as a field headland with a hedge on your left.

Keep close to the hedge on your left to avoid Kings golf course to your right. The golf course expands beyond the hedge on the left and ends on the right. The path now passes through the edge of Mill Covert. Keep close to the stream on your left.

Cross the footbridge over the stream. Carlton church tower lies straight ahead but the footpath bears left to cross the hedge on the left of the field, near a telegraph pole. Cross into the corner of the field on your left. Walk towards Carlton close to the hedge on your right to meet the road.

CARLTON *village is to your right. The church with its quaint bell tower was built in 1764 after the earlier church burnt down. The older pretty houses cluster around the church and beyond that on Barton Road is The Gate Hangs Well (and hinders none, Refresh, pay and travel on........). Just north of here at Barton in the Beans the Deacon family made and sold clocks from the mid 18th century until 1951. Many of their longcase clocks survive in museum collections and private hands. On route we pass the former school provided "for the education of poor children of the parish in AD 1847" and now a private dwelling.*

Turn left along the village street. Pass the old school and turn right along Shackerstone Walk. Pass the green and along a path to the left of Glebe Farm. The path ends at a gate. Turn sharp left to pass large barns on your right. Keep in the same direction until you reach the end of the field. Turn right and walk close to the hedge on your left.

Cross the footbridge and walk uphill with the hedge still on your left. The gate in the top corner leads you into a hedged square. Keep in the same direction with the hedge now on your right and cross another footbridge. You now have a series of very wide, open fields to cross. Keep in a straight line through the waymarked gaps across the middle of these fields. In the fourth smaller square field, head for a gate in the far left corner ($\otimes$ SK 38522 06017). Cross the footbridge.

The next field is bordered by a long stretch of woodland (Long Covert). You need to reach the far right corner of this wood where it meets Barton Lane near the isolated house. Cross the road to the left of the cottage and continue in the same direction going diagonally left across the field, keep the overhead cables and poles on your right and make for the right corner of Orange Hill Plantation.

SHACKERSTONE *station footbridge. The public footpath over the station footbridge was closed in 2008 because the bridge had become unsafe. In 2017 there is still a temporary diversion to the route (shown blue on the map).*

When the bridge is repaired, continue in the same direction across the field. Cross the railway footbridge over the station then turn right to walk alongside the canal to the road junction.

Until then, from the corner of Orange Hill Plantation the path heads northwards following the fence until you meet a stile and junction with the bridleway from Barton in the Beans. Turn left onto the concrete farm drive and follow this under the railway bridge where it meets the station drive, near the Turn Bridge over the canal, here you rejoin the usual Leicestershire Round route. (The waymarked temporary alternative route is available by the kind permission of the Crown Estate and their tenants.)

SHACKERSTONE *The railway here opened in 1873 and closed in 1970. It was then bought by enthusiasts and today runs as a tourist attraction. Like the nearby canal it carried mainly coal and minerals. Passenger traffic ended in 1931. The canal is very pretty, with its many-coloured boats. The station drive bridge over the infant River Sence is cast iron on brick pillars and offers a good view of the river passing under the canal. The motte of the 12th century castle is visible as a mound beside the canal. Nearby was Gopsall Hall where G.F Handel stayed on many occasions with his friends Humphrey and Charles Jennens. It was here in 1743 that he wrote his Messiah the words to which were penned by Charles Jennens. The Rising Sun in Shackerstone will offer mere mortals hospitality.*

Do not cross the canal Turn Bridge, pass through the handgate to join the canal towpath. Shackerstone village centre, with church and pub, lies to your left over the bridge.

Old Ivy House B&B
Congerstone
01827 881104.

SHACKERSTONE - NEWTOWN LINFORD

This section leaves the canal and passes the now exhausted coalfields of Nailstone, Bagworth and Thornton but stone quarries are still close by. The old mining eyesores have been cleared and the hills planted with trees to create the National Forest. Some houses in Bagworth still show scars of mining subsidence. From Thornton on its high hill, there are beautiful views over the Victorian reservoir and then you have rolling hills to climb approaching the Charnwood Forest. Markfield, a bustling little village has good services and buses. The section has changed dramatically since the walk was devised, woodland has replaced open fields and open views are now exchanged for the chatter of birds in the established trees.

SHACKERSTONE - NAILSTONE
(3 miles)

From Turn Bridge, Shackerstone go down to the canal towpath. Walk with the canal on your left until you are opposite the old castle mound on the far side of the canal. Turn right through a gate, cross the field and go up the waymarked steps and over the former railway line now a drive for cars so take care. Cross the footbridge over the stream and go straight ahead, under the

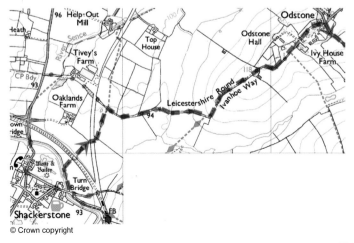

© Crown copyright

bridge of the second old railway line. Bear left across the field, meeting the field road turn right and follow this track for about a mile to Odstone. The Leicestershire Round and Ivanhoe Way will share the same route to Bagworth.

From the top of the rise you have fine views. On your left pass the ha-ha wall of Odstone Hall and continue along the drive from the hall, past Ivy House Farm. Meet the Barton road and turn right towards Barton in the Beans.

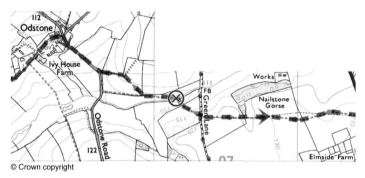
© Crown copyright

After about 350M, where the road swings right turn left and follow the field track which goes uphill for a short distance, close to the hedge on your left. Where the hedge and track turn left, bear right across the field down to the corner. Turn left into the next narrow field and gently cross the field to locate a footbridge on far side (Y SK 40163 07418). Go straight across the next little field and then move uphill diagonally left to meet Green Lane.

Cross the lane to enter an arable field. Nailstone church spire, your next goal, lies directly ahead. You need to cross huge fields, passing a big wood, Nailstone Gorse, over to your left. Keep making for the church spire until you meet the road (the A447). Take care! This is a busy road and there is little or no verge on which to wait for a gap in the fast moving traffic. (Please make a report if you feel the hedge needs a trim).

Cross the A447 and continue along the lane opposite (Vero's Lane). The lane passes the rear of houses to emerge on Main Street, beside the former Queens Head public house.

NAILSTONE *stands high on the hilly ground. The 13th century church has a fine broach spire, visible for miles. Inside there is the slab of a 1664 memorial to Thomas Corbett of Barton, once showing Thomas with his long peaked beard and in his slashed doublet and ermine collar. Thomas Corbett was Sergeant of the Pantry under four Tudor monarchs, Henry VIII, Edward VI, Mary Tudor and Elizabeth. His first wife produced 19 children in 18 years. His second wife produced two more.*

The WI Village Book records that in 1745 the Young Pretender Prince Charles Stuart rode with his highlanders to Elm Tree farm to discover from the Knowles family what support he might expect from the area. He made the decision to retreat! When it comes to describing the footpaths around Nailstone, the WI book offers - "A network of footpaths fan out over sweeping plough and grasslands providing pleasant walks through meadows garlanded with wildflowers alongside rambling streams". This is surely a memory of times gone by! Many of the wildflowers have been eradicated by the ploughing; but it is pleasant to think of them as we cross the huge prairie fields. This is former mining country. Nailstone and Bagworth collieries would once have been visible to the north of our route. The reclaimed spoil heaps are now planted with trees. Pit head winding wheels have been replaced by attractive views. In 1987 there were two inns here The Queens Head is now converted to a dwelling and the Bulls Head sadly looks a little run down.

NAILSTONE - BAGWORTH
(2 miles)

Continue along the footpath opposite Vero's Lane to pass Nailstone church on your left. At the lychgate turn left along Church Road until it bends left, take the footpath right. Keep close to the hedge on your left and pass the electricity transformer. When the hedge ends keep in the same direction, across the open field, to meet a hedge on your right. Cross another open field, ignore the path that forks off left to Crown Farm. Cross two more fields to reach the road.

© Crown copyright

Cross the road, enter the field and continue close to the hedge on your left. Go downhill to cross the stream then turn left beside the stream, along the edge of Underhills Wood. Turn right to follow a hedge on the left, this is a bridleway which offers a good track to the road at Bagworth. Continue along the road into the village.

There was once a great house at BAGWORTH. Lord Hastings who played such an important part in the Wars of the Roses and who supported Richard III, received a royal licence to fortify three great houses in Leicestershire, Ashby de la Zouch, Kirby Muxloe and Bagworth. Ashby and Kirby are both very impressive still but the Bagworth house was in ruins when Leland saw it in about 1540. Only a moat survives at Bagworth Park, north east of the village. It is easier to see the evidence of Bagworth's industrial revolution. Its mines are now closed but you can still see the evidence of the damage caused by subsidence, there are cracks in the walls of many buildings. The Bagworth Incline, where in Stephenson's time, trains were pulled up the steep hill by a steam engine at the top, now remains as a pleasant walk between hedges. The old stone church was also much damaged by mining and was rebuilt in concrete, externally an ugly building now also gone.

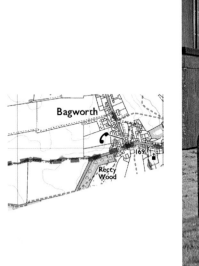

BAGWORTH - THORNTON
(1 ½ miles)

At Bagworth, pass Station Road on your left. Continue along Main Street, pass The Square on your left and turn right up Church Hill. Pass the churchyard on your left then enter a field, keep close to the hedge on your left. About half way along the field turn left through a gate to cross the cemetery. In the next field bear right

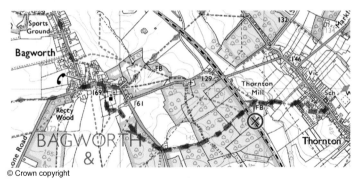

to the far corner and continue in the same direction, walking downhill across a small field to enter woodland. Follow the wide track between the trees.

Planted since the 1996 guide, which said, "in a field designated for Woodland Trust planting" The trees are now well established.

Meet the road where it crosses under the pylon lines. Cross the road to enter Bagworth Wood and continue on the wide green track. The former field boundaries are now lost as is the beckoning spire of Thornton church but the path is easy to follow with yellow topped posts. Cross a metalled path and continue to descend through the woodland to reach a railway line. (NOTE: There is a proposal 2017 to close the level crossing of the line and divert the path through a bridge further south (Y SK 45935 07783). Cross the active mineral line with care.

This was the Leicester to Swannington railway line, opened by Stephenson in 1832, the first public railway in the Midlands. There were plans to reopen the line to passengers as the Ivanhoe Line but they came to nothing.

Continue in the same direction, with the hedge on your right. Turn right and walk close to the stream on your left. Cross the footbridge over the stream and the mill race and swing left to walk through the yard of Thornton Mill, over the cobbles and past the old millstones set in the track. The track leads straight up to Main Street, Thornton but as the lane bends left our path turns right. Cross the field passing under the cables and head towards the houses. Turn left up the narrow path with a private garden on your right then right to enter the housing estate. Continue straight ahead along Hawthorn Drive which swings left to meet Main Street, opposite Thornton primary school.

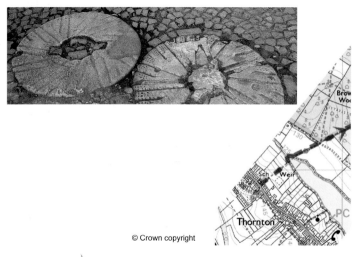

© Crown copyright

The Township of **THORNTON** is referred to in 1086. The church dates from 1189. It has a very varied and interesting interior, with medieval glass and 16th century linenfold bench ends. The great medieval door has ironwork which dates from the 13th century and is said to have come from the ruined priory of Ulverscroft. The village has two pubs which serve food and the view from the recreation ground makes this a good picnic spot. There are cottages in the village street dating from 1666. The reservoir was built in 1853 and offers some popular walks along permissive paths.

THORNTON - MARKFIELD
(2 miles)

From Thornton Main Street take the path to the right of the school which leads straight down to the beautiful Thornton reservoir. The path loops left to pass around the head of the reservoir then continues on the original line up the hill with a hedge on your left.

Ignore the path off left but take the stile a few metres later to cross the hedge. Now continue up hill with the hedge on your right, ignore a second path off to the left.

At the brow of the hill woodland is replaced by open fields on your right. As you start to descend look for a gate on the right hand hedge. Take this gate into the open field and continue now with the hedge on your left.

Drop down the field to a stile by a field gate (⊗ SK 47555 08693). (Here a stile offers an escape from the woodland path if you missed the gate). Continue up the hill across the open field to a gate.

That was a brief respite from woodland because here the path continues between trees on a well defined path dropping again to cross a stream at a crossing of paths. Continue gently up as the roar of traffic becomes deafening. The path leaves the wood at a corner and the source of the noise becomes apparent as cars and lorries thunder past on the motorway.

Continue cutting across the corners of the next two fields. Turn left to walk beside the motorway on your right. Turn right and go under the motorway bridge.

Follow the hedged farm road, ignoring two paths off to the left. After about 250 metres leave the track through a gate on the right then immediately pass through another gate to the left. Pass a large oak tree between the second and third fields. The final field is a water meadow and may be wet, keep to the surfaced path. Go between the houses, and bear left out of the cul-de-sac, up Croft Way to Forest Road. Turn right for a short distance along Forest Road, then left into Main Street, Markfield.

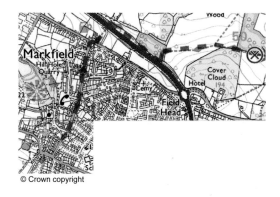

© Crown copyright

MARKFIELD *has an interesting mixture of buildings. The main village street is rather straggly with a mix of domestic architecture. The name indicates that this was once a settlement of the Mercians but the village shows little of this history. The former Miners' Institute reminds us of more recent activity as does Hill Hole the remains of mining, now a nature reserve and viewpoint. The Altar Stones site, managed by Leicestershire and Rutland Wildlife Trust, was the rim of an ancient volcano. Markfield, a gateway to the Forest, provides shops, pubs, parking spaces and a reasonable bus service.*

MARKFIELD - NEWTOWN LINFORD
(3 miles)

From the top of Main Street, Markfield, take the right hand fork, past the No Entry sign. Turn right along the Leicester Road and turn left at the footpath sign near the bus stop. Follow the metalled subway under the A50 dual carriageway.

Turn left then immediately right, walk along the sloping bank close to the hedgerow, the main A50 road is on your right. Continue onto the wide open verge then by the 'Reduce Speed Now' sign, bear left down the short slope with a hedge on your left. Keep left along a well walked path between brambles to a bridge and gate.

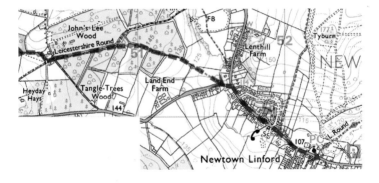

Cross the field to pass north of Cover Cloud Wood, keep the wood on your right. When the wood ends continue with a new plantation on the left. Turn right over concrete bridge (Y SK 50090 10440) and through a gate then immediately left to continue in the same direction with hedge now on your left.

Tangle Trees farmhouse is ahead, bear right along the fence line. At a well signed gate turn left continue along the driveway. Pass the house and outbuildings on your left and continue in the same direction through the gate to pass John's Lee Wood on your left. Continue straight ahead with plantations on both sides.

After a half mile (1km) the wood ends on your right, after about another 100 metres turn right over a bridge and through a gate into the field. Turn left, with hedge on your left. After the next gate move diagonally right downhill towards the corner and road.

At the road (Markfield Lane) turn left to the junction and turn right into Newtown Linford. Bradgate Park entrance lies three quarters of a mile along the road through the pretty village of Newtown Linford.

If you started the walk from page one congratulations you can now purchase a cloth badge to mark your achievement. See the LFA website for details.